THE FEARLESS ADVISOR'S PLAYBOOK

MARK HOLTON OAM   MATTHEW FEEHAN

THE FEARLESS ADVISOR'S PLAYBOOK

7 Steps to Drive Your Firm Beyond Compliance

First published in 2026 by Dean Publishing
PO Box 119
Mt. Macedon, Victoria, 3441
Australia
deanpublishing.com

Cataloguing-in-Publication Data
National Library of Australia
Title: The Fearless Advisor's Playbook
ISBN: 978-1-7643723-8-1
Category: Business Management/Accounting/Advising

*To the accounting industry — remember
to be fearless. Take that first step.*

CONTENTS

FOREWORD

For more than three decades I've known Mark Holton, and over those years we've often found ourselves speaking at the same events for the accounting profession; sometimes together, sometimes simply sharing the same stage on different sessions.

Across all that time, one theme has remained remarkably consistent.

Accountants are uniquely positioned to help business owners shape their futures.

In fact, many years ago, when I was running the Accountants' Boot Camp programs (attended by more than 17,000 accountants around the world) I began every event with a simple observation:

"Your job is not to report on history. It is to help your selected clients create it."

That single idea captures the enormous opportunity that sits inside this profession.

But here's the uncomfortable truth.

Most accountants already *know* this.

David Maister famously described the accountant as the 'Trusted Advisor'. The concept has been around for decades. Yet many firms still remain anchored to a model built around compliance work, time sheets and reporting on what has already happened.

So the issue has never been awareness. The issue has been boldness. Or being 'FEARLESS' as Mark and Matthew describe and position it brilliantly.

And right now, that model is being challenged faster than ever before.

Processes that once required significant manual effort can now be handled at what seems like break-neck speed through AI-based systems. And by the way, that shift will never be slower than it is today. Think about that.

For example, as I write this foreword during a short break in Tokyo, a new AI application has just been announced claiming to autonomously prepare complex partnership returns—including the reasoning behind the work.

AI systems are getting better at structured reasoning all the time. Clients expect faster turnaround and clearer value. And finding humans to do compliance work isn't getting easier.

When those forces converge, business models change.

So the critical question becomes this: now that compliance is automated, what will your firm be known for?

Or perhaps more importantly: What will your firm be designed for?

Technology alone does not create great firms. People do.

Specifically, people who are prepared to step forward, engage deeply with their clients, ask better questions, and help those clients navigate the future.

That is the real opportunity for accountants today. And it requires courage. And that brings us directly to this book.

Mark Holton has spent more than four decades helping accounting firms move from compliance toward advisory work. Over that time he has seen what works, what doesn't, and why so many firms hesitate at the very moment when they should move forward.

Together with Matt Feehan who has implemented these ideas successfully within his own practice, they give you something incredibly valuable here: a practical roadmap for turning the idea of advisory into a real and profitable part of a firm.

Importantly, this is not theory. It's experience.

The stories, frameworks and insights in these pages reflect thousands of client conversations and many years spent helping firms make the transition from reporting on the past to shaping the future. And that transition is exactly what this profession needs.

Because when accountants fully embrace their role as advisors, something remarkable happens.

Businesses grow faster. Decisions improve. Owners gain clarity. And the relationship between accountant and client becomes far more meaningful.

In short, accountants stop simply recording business history—and start helping create it.

This book helps you take that step.

And as you take that step (because take it you must) remember these words of Andy Grove, the CEO and Chairman of Intel until his death in 2016: "Success breeds complacency. Complacency breeds failure. Only the paranoid survive."

For 'paranoid' read "FEARLESS".

So read this brilliant book with curiosity. And most importantly, act on it.

Because the opportunity in front of the accounting profession right now is enormous.

Actually, let me re-write that line: "the opportunity in front of you right now is enormous.

Enjoy the book.

And go create some history.

PAUL DUNN

Co-Founder of B1G1

REVOLUTIONISE YOUR INCOME, LIFESTYLE, AND CLIENT RELATIONSHIPS WITH A BUSINESS ADVISORY SERVICE

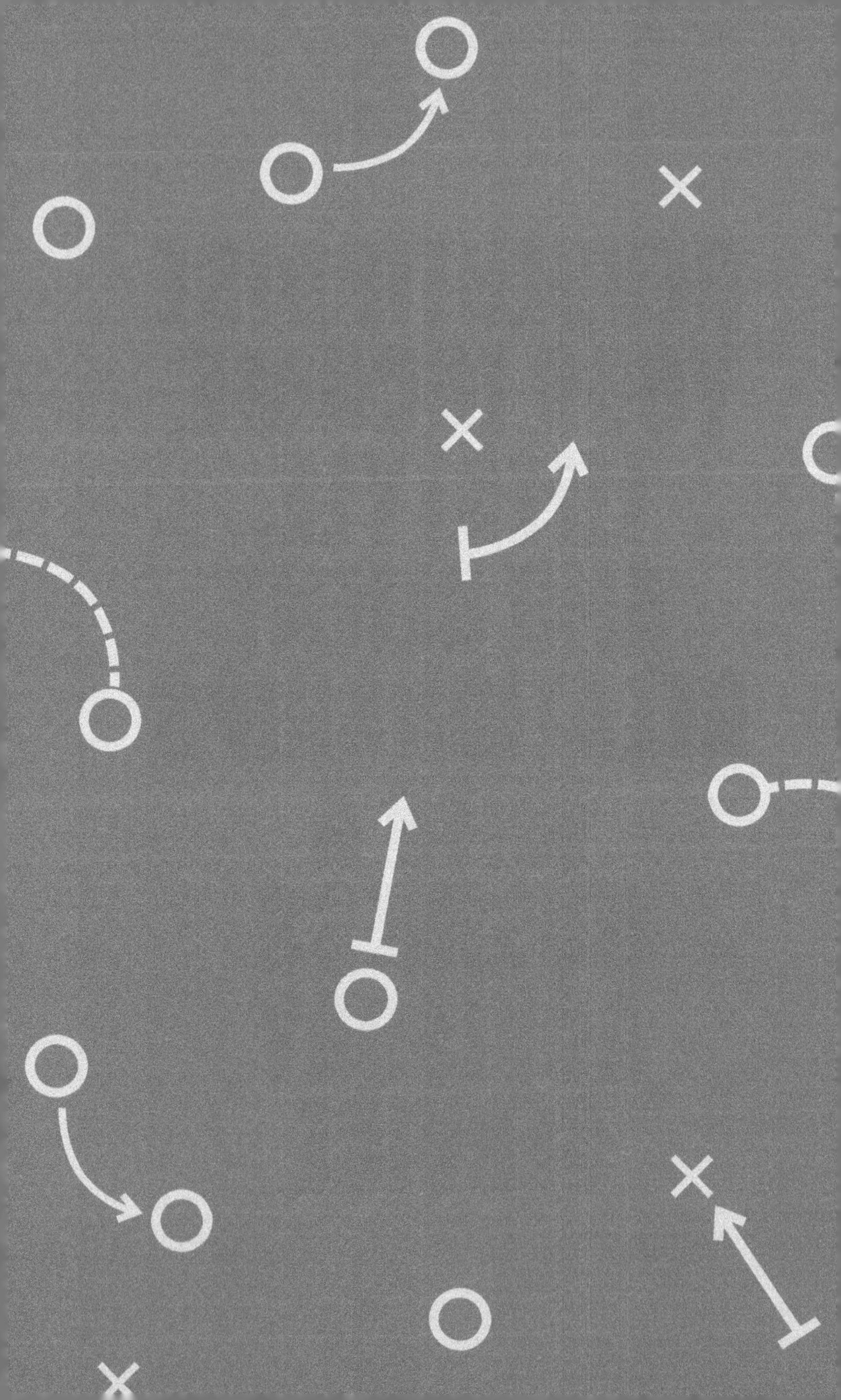

Research shows that business owners in the SME (small to medium-sized enterprise) sector are crying out for quality advice to help them run their businesses.

In theory, no one is better placed to offer a business owner advice than their accountants. But if you're focused on compliance, you won't be in a position to support those clients with the knowledge, experience, and resources they need to make a tangible difference to their cash flow and profitability and, ultimately, increase the value of their businesses.

Many firms would like to offer a business advisory service, and some make a tentative start in the right direction. But in our experience, only around 10 percent are successful within a reasonable timeframe.

Mark Holton has spent over 40 years helping firms successfully implement advisory services across Australia, UK, New Zealand, Singapore, Canada, and the US.

Matt Feehan has walked the walk, establishing an advisory division in his previous firm that was able to generate $500,000 in fees in the first full 12 months. He subsequently started a new business advisory firm, with compliance as the secondary focus.

We want to help you do the same. Why? Because we believe business advisory plays a critical role in the future of the profession and offers enormous opportunities for the people who work in it. But most of all, because we know from firsthand experience that a successful advisory model enables businesses to prosper – not just bringing financial and professional rewards to advisory firms and their partners, but also empowering their clients to grow and thrive.

Our hands-on experience mentoring firms through the transition to successful advisory work led us to develop the seven-step Enabler™ process. This framework is a step-by-step guide to evolving from a compliance-focused firm to one that gains a substantial percentage of its income from advisory work.

The Fearless Advisor's Playbook outlines the seven steps of the Enabler™ process, includes some war stories, and discusses our success in assisting other firms to build successful advisory businesses. By the end of this book, you'll know enough to get started in creating a business advisory implementation plan for your firm, approaching each step with fearless determination.

Even with a proven framework behind you, moving into advisory work is a complex undertaking. It's one that often challenges and stretches you personally and professionally, and requires a high degree of commitment from the firm and its partners. You'll invariably encounter obstacles along the way, which may slow your momentum and dampen your enthusiasm. But that doesn't mean you should give up. Becoming an advisory-based practice really does have the potential to revolutionise your income, your lifestyle, and your client relationships.

Mark: Having the tenacity to push through the obstacles is what it takes to reap the rewards.

Matt: Everyone wants to go skydiving until they're sitting on the edge of the plane. Plan properly, and the parachute will open.

SEVERAL GREAT REASONS TO OFFER BUSINESS ADVISORY SERVICES

When you implement business advisory services successfully, you have the potential to transform your business, enabling you to:

- Do less work for more money
- Even out your cash flow across the full financial year
- Increase key clients' worth to your practice over both the short and long term (as a client's business grows under your guidance, so too do your fees)
- Differentiate yourself to gain new clients and

incentivise existing ones to keep doing business with you instead of shifting to cheaper, compliance-focused competitors

- Have more meaningful relationships with your clients (and make them more inclined to refer new business to you, and less likely to switch providers)
- Spend your time doing more satisfying and personally rewarding work – and attract and retain quality team members who have the same aspirations

Don't get us wrong – you and your firm are likely pretty comfortable as you are, and at the moment, the sky probably won't fall in if you decide an advisory model isn't for you. But there's no question that the revenue streams the industry has traditionally relied on for its bread-and-butter fees are coming under pressure.

Over the past few years, we've personally observed SME clients becoming better educated about financial matters, and more aggressive in choosing their accountants. Coinciding with the advent of easy-to-use cloud accounting software and low-cost outsourcing options, this has led to compliance work becoming increasingly price-sensitive and commoditised.

GIVEN HOW MANY SMES ARE LOOKING FOR EXTERNAL ADVISORS TO HELP THEM RUN AND GROW THEIR BUSINESSES, OFFERING BUSINESS ADVISORY SERVICES MAKES GOOD SENSE AND CAN FIRMLY ESTABLISH YOU AS THE FIRM OF CHOICE IN THE MINDS OF YOUR CURRENT AND FUTURE CLIENTS.

If you'd like to earn more money without working more hours and while enjoying more rewarding relationships with your clients, then we believe implementing an advisory model warrants your serious consideration.

Mark: The key issue preventing firms from succeeding in the business advisory arena is an unwillingness to create the time needed to implement the services effectively. If you're going to make it work for you, you need to stop thinking of advisory services as an add-on and start considering them core to your business offering.

Matt: It's far easier to increase the value of your current clients than to try and sell compliance services to new clients on the street. Additionally, the best talent is looking for varied work, rather than finishing a tax return to start the next tax return. Accepting the challenge can make your clients happier, your team happier, and you and your firm wealthier.

IS IT REALLY WORTH THE HASSLE?

We can't predict how much you stand to gain by offering business advisory services. Every firm is different, and so too is every practitioner within it. Not every firm or every individual is well suited to specialist advisory work.

What we can tell you is we've worked with small and medium-sized firms that have added hundreds of thousands of dollars to their revenue – not necessarily by suddenly snaring a blue-chip client from the big end of town, but by systematically increasing their volume of existing engagements, often from within their existing fee base. Accounting firms also tell us that offering business advisory services helps them get better staff on board.

Perhaps the most rewarding aspect of all is that your advisory work stands to have very real, tangible benefits for your clients. Business surveys show that many SMEs are faced with declining revenues and profits, increased pressure on their pricing and margins, escalating labour and fuel costs, and adverse exchange rates.[1] Helping them navigate this increasingly complex and competitive business environment and improve their business performance and value will be some of the most challenging yet satisfying work you could ever hope to do.

WHAT WILL IT COST?

Starting a business advisory service isn't a decision to make lightly. The financial gains you stand to make are significant, but you'll need to make some sacrifices in order to achieve them. You'll probably need to invest time and money in upskilling your team and upgrading your software. Crucially, you'll probably also need to free someone up to champion the project, and the right person may be a partner or senior accountant who's responsible for a significant percentage of your existing billings. Then there are the complexities and challenges of promoting a new business culture, complete with updated processes and fresh priorities.

Most importantly, you'll need to be prepared to push yourself out of your comfort zone – and to bring your colleagues along for the ride. It can be confronting to push through the discomfort of initiating more intimate relationships with your clients and giving them advice without initially knowing what the consequences will be. In other words, you'll need to go out on a limb, both personally and professionally.

Some firms aren't prepared to take those risks.

In our experience, many firms that take the initial steps towards an advisory model fail to make it all the way through to successful implementation. Which means if you're driven to succeed and willing to commit the necessary time, funds, and personnel to make it happen, you'll stand out from the herd.

Your advisory work stands to have very real, tangible benefits for your clients.

INTRODUCING THE ENABLER™ SEVEN STEPS TO SUCCESS

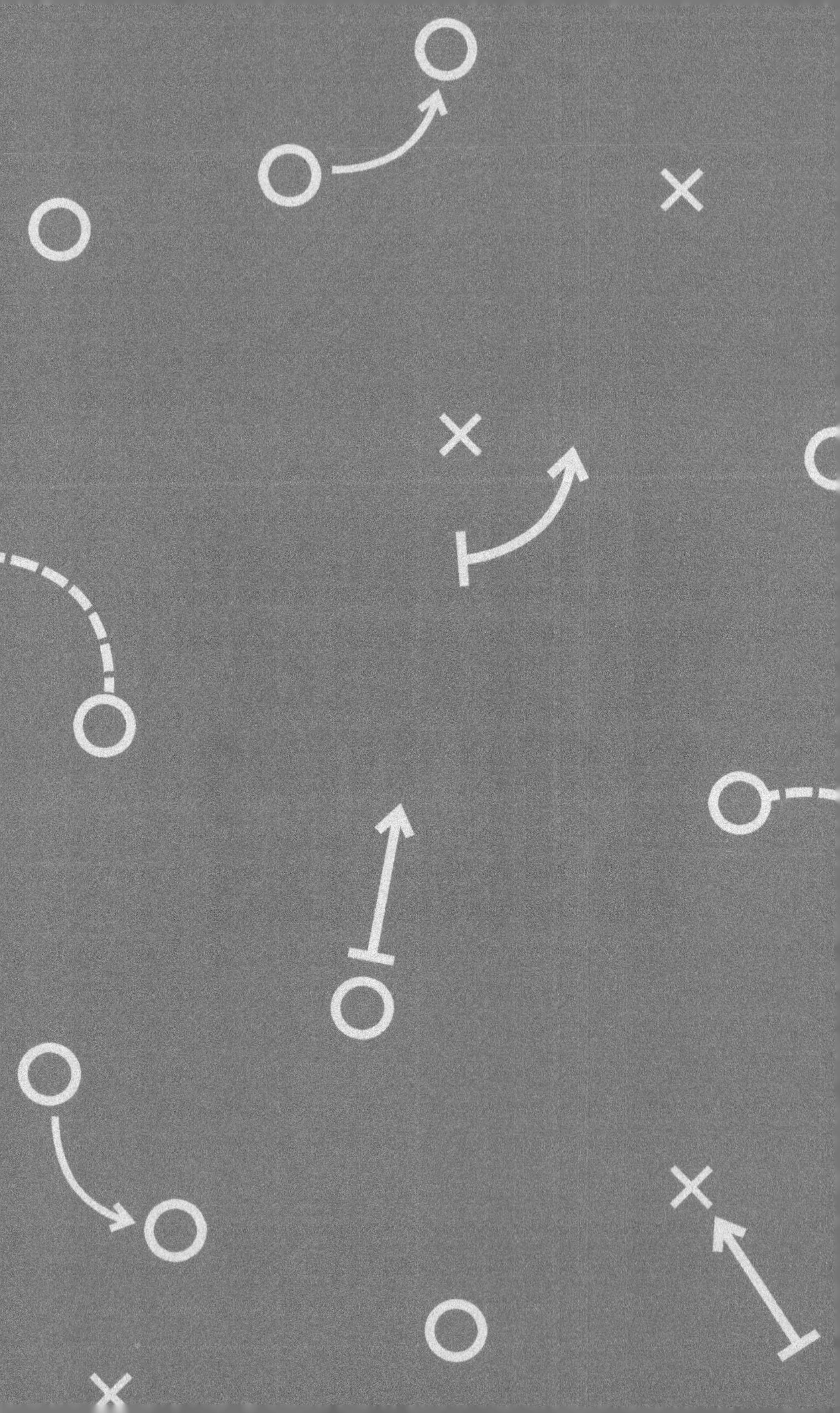

We've developed our exclusive Enabler™ process to help you overcome all the obstacles to success and make the most of every opportunity. In the pages to follow, we'll guide you through the seven steps to successful implementation.

MARK'S TIPS FOR NEW PLAYERS

Don't attempt to roll out advisory services across your whole fee base at once, and don't start with your A-class clients. Instead, identify three existing clients you can use as case studies to build your confidence. Look for clients whom you have the closest relationship with.

Choose them based on how easy the clients are to work with and how readily they take advice. In our experience, the best candidates for this initial phase are those for whom a small change to a key driver, such as profit margins or number of collection days, will create a rapid and measurable cash flow benefit.

Spend as much time as necessary reviewing your clients' financial records and preparing for your initial discussions with them before actually meeting them. Your goal is to interact with them authentically and authoritatively, and in a way that empowers them to trust and engage with you.

Once you've got those three under your belt, the next three advisory clients should be considered practice clients to help build your confidence. After that, select four more as revenue builders. By the time you've managed engagements with all ten, you'll be on your way.

We've found that many firms fail at advisory

services due to a lack of confidence. It does require courage to get out of your comfort zone initially, and to persist until it becomes second nature. That's why our Business Advisory Enabler™ program includes extensive role-playing sessions to help you overcome your nerves and prepare you for those initial client meetings that can otherwise make you feel like going before the firing squad.

The seven most common reasons for failure to implement business advisory services are:

1. Lack of time
2. Lack commitment and capacity (the two Cs)
3. Not having enough confidence to deliver business advisory services and not being prepared to get out of your comfort zone
4. Not selecting the right clients to work with
5. Not having a practice champion or the right staff in place
6. Not providing adequate training and development for team members
7. Not developing a business advisory implementation plan

Now that we've established why transitioning to advisory services is crucial, let's delve into the first step: preparing your practice for this transformative journey.

STEP 1

PREPARE YOUR FIRM FOR SUCCESS

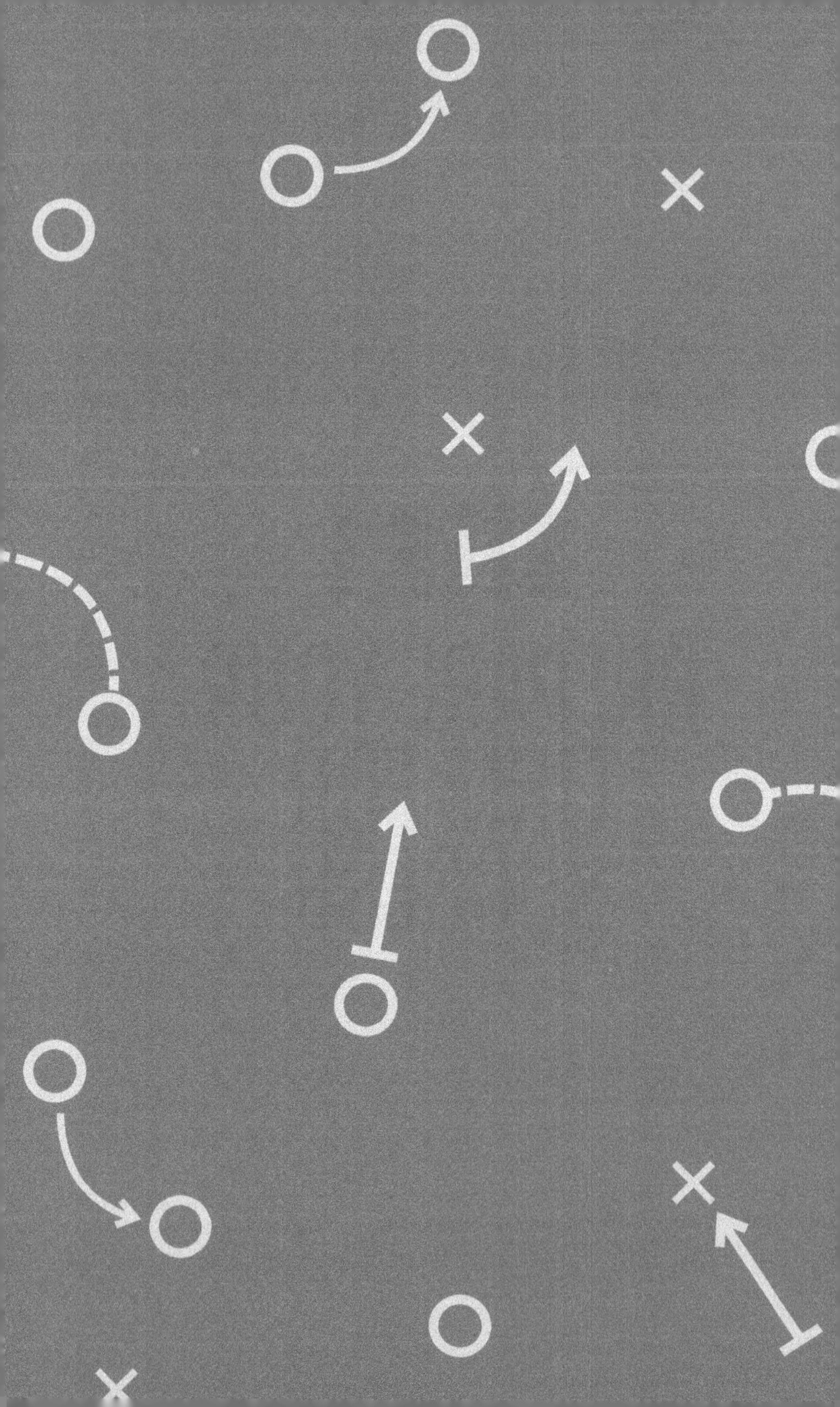

If you've decided you're up for the challenge of business advisory work, the single most important piece of advice we can give you is this: you're not going to succeed if you don't have a solid, proven implementation plan such as the Enabler™ Seven Steps to Success approach in place, and the resourcing and capacity to systematically roll it out. In our experience, you'll also need to nominate someone to champion the project typically a partner or senior accountant. Ideally, your project champion should be someone who's strong and determined, and has the influence and leadership qualities required to push through the personal discomforts that may make some individuals in the firm hesitant to proceed or to step up to the plate.

With that in mind, some key steps we recommend you consider at the outset include:

- **A proven implementation plan:** Even if you don't work with the Enabler™ system, we urge you not to proceed down the advisory path without a plan. We've seen too many firms try and fail, and we know that failure can be not only demoralising but also very, very expensive.

- **Increase capacity:** Setting up a business advisory service isn't something you can squeeze in around the edges of a busy compliance practice. One of the first things your plan should cover is how you're going to increase your firm's and staff members' capacity, and free up the time of those who will be most crucial to your success. This might involve hiring more team members, delegating work others can do, improving your internal processes and staff training to boost efficiency, upgrading your IT hardware and systems, or even letting go of some clients whom you no longer want to work with (perhaps by increasing your prices to encourage them to go elsewhere).

- **Resourcing:** Have you got the right staff, in the right roles, with the right decision-making power to dedicate themselves to business advisory engagements? If you're considering taking on business advisory and its implementation yourself, do you have a succession plan for handing over your existing responsibilities? Learn how to hire with this model in mind, ensuring you gather the best team to elevate your business.

- **Targets:** Over the years, we've observed that the firms that set themselves solid targets are the ones most likely to succeed. For example, you may set a goal that in 2 years your advisory income from the first ten clients you introduce to the service will reach 50 percent of your compliance billing to them. A concrete goal like this will also help you gain buy-in from your partners and co-workers.

- **Accountability:** Aside from the list of action-based steps involved in implementing your plan, make sure you've considered how you're going to keep yourselves accountable to your commitment. If you need help with that, consider enrolling in Mark Holton's Business Advisory Enabled™ program, which has been specially developed to keep you on track to achieve your goals.

- **Systems:** There are a number of software tools that will enhance your advisory work – some of which we'll discuss in more detail later. But the systems and processes involved in successfully implementing an advisory service go beyond IT. How will you identify suitable clients to offer your advisory services to? How will you track your success rate? How will you price your services? How will you ensure each opportunity – now and in the future — is followed up for optimal outcomes for both the firm and the client? How will you ensure all relevant people on the team receive the ongoing training they need to develop and improve their advisory skills?

FAIL TO PLAN, PLAN TO FAIL

As Eleanor Roosevelt once said, "It takes as much energy to wish as it does to plan." Instead of spending your days wishing your business could take on more advisory services, now's the time to get the ball rolling and plan your way to fruition. As previously mentioned, we advise not to dive into business advisory without a solid plan in place. As with anything in life, being prepared encourages ideas to bloom, and by planning out your first steps into this field, it's much easier to plant roses along your path to success. Not only will you be on the pathway, but you'll have developed the first service you can roll out to your clients.

Mark is a firm believer in preparedness when it comes to the very early stages of using the seven steps. He recommends you complete four steps to ensure the success of your plan:

1. Structure the firm to get the right systems, resources, processes, and people who possess the capacity and commitment to succeed.
2. Develop the service infrastructure:
   » What are you selling?
   » How much will it cost to deliver?
   » How much will the service sell for?
   » How will you package the service?
   » How do you explain to a prospective client in a manner they feel is beneficial to them and will inspire them to sign on to your services?
3. Create a strong and committed client engagement model and follow that model for all advisory jobs.
4. Develop delivery models in a systemised and scalable fashion. Find the right person to champion and complete the right tasks for the right salary.

NOMINATE YOUR CHAMPION

So, how do you go about nominating your champion? Firstly, and most importantly, you should find someone who's interested in this type of work. Someone who wants to be a financial storyteller! Your champion will be someone who's up for the challenge and naturally thrives on making strong connections. The hunger for creating rich relationships with your clients matters more than technical compliance expertise.

If you're finding it tricky to nominate someone based on these criteria, a partner or senior member of your team would be your next option. The key is personality and the yearning to pivot from their usual duties. You're looking for the glue – the one who, although they may not be technically strong, shows skill in client management and already has a great relationship with your base.

> "YOUR CHAMPION WILL BE A FINANCIAL STORYTELLER WHO WANTS TO ENGAGE WITH YOUR CLIENTS, TAKE THEM ON A JOURNEY, SHARE IN THEIR STORIES, AND ULTIMATELY GET A REAL KICK OUT OF HELPING THEM ACHIEVE THEIR GOALS."

It's important that your champion has the passion for human connection and the drive to advise your clients to, in turn, champion their own business goals. You need someone who's determined to exchange roles so they don't eventually return to what's comfortable and familiar. Just as you may feel you're taking a chance, the person you nominate should feel as though they themselves are striving for the next step in their career.

Business advisory, after all, is about looking forward and never glancing back. It's implementing a plan for what will happen, rather than the usual method in accounting of assessing what has already occurred. When looking towards the future, your champion will need to be fearless in the face of the unknown. Not only that, but also be able to support your client as they take a new step forward.

Matt knows the role of the champion firsthand. He took on this role initially within his business, showing that successfully implementing the seven steps is achievable. As he gained traction in this role, he knew he had to diversify and nominate a champion of his own. He used strategy where team members aimed to meet a $20,000 target outside of tax-related work each month, with results displayed on a 'wins board', creating a clear picture of who was suited to the role.

Ultimately, creating clear goals for your champion gives them accountability while allowing you to measure their performance in line with your financial outcomes.

WINS BOARD

DATE	CLIENT	JOB	$ VALUE	RESPONSIBLE	COMPLETED
01/04/2024	JOE BLOGGS COFFEE	BENCHMARK REPORT	2,500	MF	Y
15/04/2024	ABC PTY LTD	STRATEGY DAY	10,000	MF/MH	N
		TOTAL:	12,500		

The following table can help you identify your ideal nominees within your business and whittle down the top employees to find your champion. Fill it out and, using the guide in this section of the book, note their strength to determine the best person for the role.

NOMINEES	STRENGTHS	
	PEOPLE PERSON	
	TALKATIVE	
	INQUISITIVE	
	PROBLEM SOLVER	
	SEEKING CLIENT TIME	
	ACTIVE LISTENER	
CHAMPION:		

Once you have your champion, you need to begin the process of working business advisory into their new role. You can allocate anything from 2 hours per week to having them work on this full time. However, it's important to plan this out in line with the services you choose to offer in this space. Great planning and capacity management is the key to succeeding at this step.

Watch the video:

How to Choose Your
Business Advisory Champion

WHAT'S THE PLAN?

Matt's first tip is to make sure you take the time to sit down and plan your strategy, especially before looking into software that can aid you along the way. To build the time to look into your KPIs for the week, for example, if you have a goal of 80 percent of your KPI per week going to billable hours, nominate 20 percent of that 80 to go towards business advisory. It's advantageous to break it down and understand the numbers of your own business so you can fully understand your capacity and create the best strategy.

Mark explains you don't need to put the cart before the horse when it comes to judging your business' capacity to implement the seven-step system. Purchasing all the potentially useful software without assessing your services and which clients would benefit from business advisory can lead to a dead end. Immersing yourself in the needs of your clientele and strategising on how to present your services so your clients engage with them is the best way to ensure your horse is saddled before linking up your cart. Yee haw!

Mark notes that there are four key elements to a successful advisory firm:

1. **Structure.** If you don't have time, you don't have capacity, and therefore it's not advised to try something new and time-consuming. If you have 100 clients and don't have the capacity to take on 101, then you need to reassess if the seven steps are right for you at this time in your financial journey.

2. **Infrastructure.** It's time to ask yourself some hard-hitting questions.

- » How am I going to sell my services?
- » Who will I be selling them to?
- » What services will I offer?
- » How will I price them?
- » How do I explain to the client in a manner that's palatable for them?
- » Do I package them?
- » How much will they cost me to deliver?
- » How can I do this in the most efficient way?

3. **Engagement.** Your enthusiasm for business advisory should be expressed to the client in a way that's both informative and exciting. It's great to explain to your client that this is on par with the services you offer in the scope of tax and compliance.

4. **Delivery Models.** If you purchase software without knowing how to deliver it effectively to your clients, the purchase becomes redundant. This is why, to be successful, it's important to ensure you get the methodology correct so you know who to deliver to and what to deliver.

TIME TO TRAIN!

Once you have your champion and plan in place, your next move should be deciding how your staff are to approach implementing advisory to your clients. Training is imperative, as your staff may have zero experience in this field (this book could be a great tool! *wink*).

The implementation phase in business advisory is where the training program comes to life. During this stage, you should consider the timeline, employee engagement, learning KPI goals, and related resources (facilities, equipment, software, and so on). Participant progress should be monitored during training to ensure the program is effective.

When delving into business advisory, the four key steps to training staff are:

1. **Tell them:** Give your staff a guide as to how you see business advisory working as the new frontier of your business. Tell them what you expect from their participation and enthusiasm for this project. Explain the client base you'll be offering these services to and why you've chosen those particular clients. This gives your staff

insight into what's expected of them from both senior staff and clients.

2. **Show them:** The best way to train staff in business advisory is to show them the level of personalisation and passion you have for your clients. Show them that the main priority in offering this service is to connect on a human level and provide the best possible advice for your clients. Show them how they can harness that advice to achieve financial goals for both your business and your clients.

3. **They do it:** Now's the time to take a step back and allow your staff to show you what they've learnt from their training. Monitor and engage if questions arise; however, autonomy is a great asset when it comes to staff learning from both their mistakes and successes.

4. **You review it:** In any area of business, feedback is essential to improving and sharpening skills. Through your guidance and constructive critique, staff members can gain a greater understanding of your expectations.

There's no science when it comes to determining if you have the right staff in the right roles. The best way to decide is to give your staff time to succeed, matched with a high level of support and solid training.

Mark reflects on an accounting firm based in Western Australia that created space within their staff for advisory services. While the firm wanted to dip a toe in business advisory, they realised their current internal resources were better spent on compliance and existing work. As a solution, they reached out to a young accountant they knew from Perth who had a degree in finance. Despite the accountant's qualification in compliance services (taxation) and inexperience in business advisory, this staff member held a tenacity and enthusiasm for new experiences. The object was to employ someone whom they wouldn't drag back into compliance work when things got busy within the taxation portion of the business. This freed up the staff member to work solely in business advisory and, therefore, hone their skills to become an integral part of the team.

If you're struggling to nominate a champion, hiring someone to fill the role would work best for you.

THE J-CURVE THEORY: EXPECT THE UNEXPECTED

Matt uses a concept called the 'J-curve theory', popularised by Ian Bremmer's book *The J Curve*, which can be utilised when taking the first leap into expanding your business to include advisory services.[2]

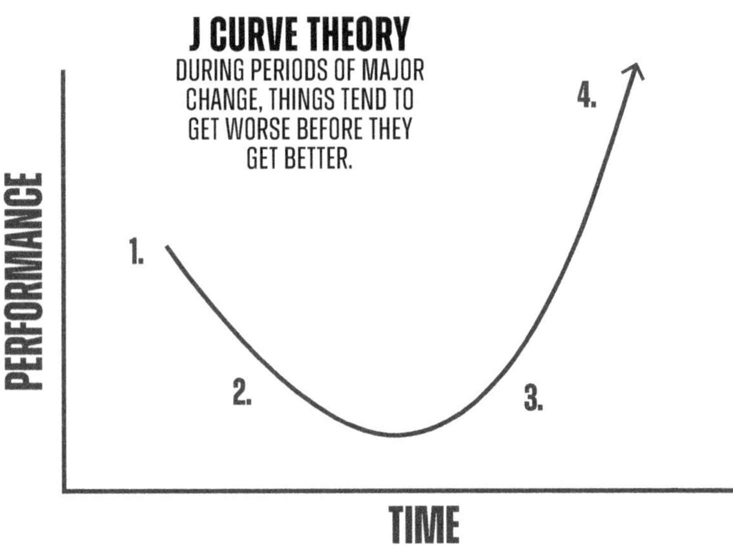

1. Where you are — a good position, but the status quo.

2. Investment in the strategy — this investment can be time, money, initial lost productivity through training and trial and error.

3. Confidence in service — efficiency gains gain now be seen by operators, confidence in the system increase by operators/clients.

4. Where you want to be — operators are able to sell to clients comfortable as they are confident they can deliver. Processes have been refined to ensure the service is being rolled out efficiently.

Matt personally identifies with this theory, as it leans into the notion that it's never good or bad news that interrupts business, but rather it's unexpected news. However, if you're expecting the unexpected, you'll be well equipped for the initial adjustment to the interruption, and it may even have a positive impact on your business.

It all begins with wanting to pivot from the status quo. When it comes to accounting, your services are needed every year. Clients flock around tax time, and although you know they'll return like clockwork, you should thirst for ways to elevate your business. While you may be in a 'good' position now, it's all about disrupting the status quo to achieve more for your business and your clients in the long run.

In the beginning stages, managing your investment is key, as you may have to tailor your expectations and be realistic about your output. You may experience an initial loss, as the J-curve theory explains; however, it's from this vantage point that you can discover what is or isn't working for your business. From reduced financial output to the time spent training staff, and even managing errors, this part of the curve is expected and should be managed logically.

As the J begins its natural ascension, both your and your clients' confidence in your services grows. Your efficiency and passion for what you're offering get fine-tuned and packaged in a way that represents your business and appeals to your clients. By creating confidence and understanding, especially after the learning period that precedes this point in the process, you become better equipped to plan for errors, manage your staff, and engage your clients.

Finally, the J reaches its greatest height! This is where you want to be. Your champion and any staff trained in advisory work are well versed and ready to work with your clients to manage their portfolios and provide stellar financial advice. Your staff are as confident to advise your clients as your clients are that they can deliver.

Your success hinges on working through the curve and experiencing the roses and thorns that come with branching out from your usual services. It's all about staying the course and managing your expectations as you begin this exciting journey of expansion. As Ronan Keating famously sang, "Life is a rollercoaster, just gotta ride it!"

CASE STUDY: FROM STRUGGLE TOWN TO PROFIT PARADISE

Matt was working closely providing business advisory to a plumber who was struggling, working 80-hour weeks, with no cash in the business. The plumber had reached the point where working for someone else as an employee would have been better than maintaining the business. In his mind, the issue was his inability to find another plumber to join his team. However, after Matt examined his debtor days, the plumber realised he had no time for administration because he was constantly on the tools, which resulted in 6-month delays in issuing invoices and having no time or energy to chase those still unpaid.

Matt encouraged him to engage an administration service as a contractor to get the proper procedures implemented and get some funds back into his account. This saved him the cost of hiring an employee in the initial period, even though the contractor was more expensive on a direct basis. This, in turn, eventually led to an employee being hired to take over the admin contractor's role. The business now has a balance of $300,000 to $400,000 per month and has paid the first dividend ($100,000) in 7 years.

In this case, Matt's advice proved valuable to his client, guiding him to elevate and restructure his business to generate profit through engaging administrative services. The client was able to sit down with Matt and find the best path forward. Although, at first, the plumber had to front the funds to get the business in order, in the long run, the financial risk was worth the reward. This has led to monthly management meetings for Matt's firm.

CLICKING WITH CLIENTS

One of the most important parts of the seven steps is choosing the right clients to partner with for business advisory services. A great place to start is by selecting a client whom you have an established, positive relationship with. Someone who hasn't issued complaints for any fee increases or deadline extensions. A client who's understanding, appreciative, and has a thirst for collaborating to elevate their business.

How to begin? Matt says to start small. Reach out to a client of your choice and ask them to meet up for a coffee and a chat. Engage with them about how their business is going. You can even go with some prepared questions, but it's a good idea to walk in with the expectation that if you leave with nothing but a better relationship with the client, that's also a win.

Work identifies itself. There will be clients who've been asking the types of questions that lend themselves to your advisory services. They may have been asking about what else their business could take on to generate more revenue, or perhaps they've confided they've had a tough few months. It's up to you to identify which clients will respond favourably to this new service you're offering.

Who not to pick? It's best to steer clear of clients who've had issues with recent compliance work or had a niggle with a recent engagement of services. In Matt's experience, they won't be interested for at least 12 months. With clients such as these, rebuilding trust in your core service allows you to gain back their trust. Once you rebuild trust, you may find that these clients turn to you for advisory work, as a large part of your new offering is based on human connection and relationships built off the back of trust.

Once your clientele has been selected, you can begin to track your success rate and gauge interest. Tracking your clients' experience from initial interest all the way to their honest feedback is worth its weight in gold when it comes to achieving success with this step. Here are some tips to help you track the client experience:

- Create a spreadsheet.
- Start with a 'leads' sheet and track any conversation with your clients that could lead to an advisory service. You'll learn as much from clients who say 'no' as you will from those who say 'yes'.
- Take an active approach. Work with your champion to ensure they're engaging your clients and putting forth their passion for your service.
- Identify 5 to 10 clients whose opinions you trust.
- Ask those clients for their feedback and encourage an open and honest line of communication so they'll give their genuine thoughts about your services.
- Explain to those clients your goal of wanting to help business owners and ask their opinion on what they believe would add the most value when it comes to enacting that help.

With your internal team aligned and ready, it's time to turn our focus outward – towards unlocking the potential within your client relationships.

STEP 2

UNLOCK YOUR CLIENTS' NEEDS

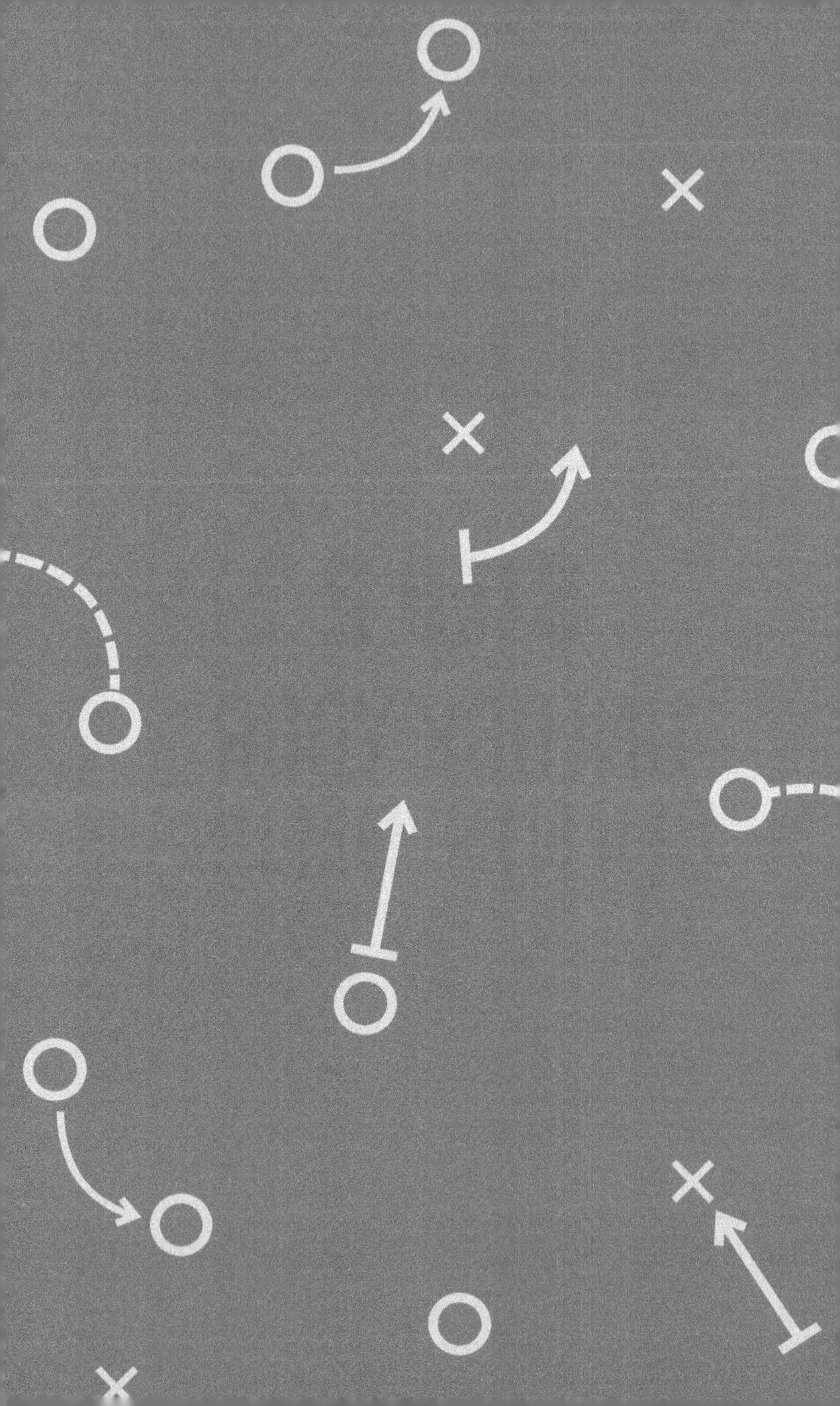

You can't service your clients effectively unless you know what they need and want. Business advisory definitely isn't a one-size-fits-all proposition!

It all begins with taking the time to study your clients' needs and working with them one on one to identify how your advice can have a lasting and dynamic impact on their businesses. You'll need to start from the top, and delving into your clients' strengths and weaknesses is the best way to begin.

As with perfecting any craft, confidence comes from practice and repetition. One technique we use with our clients is to conduct mock needs reviews. In some sessions, the client manager takes the role of the client, and others interview them (an approach that helps the client manager empathise with the client and often highlights particular areas where help is needed). In other sessions, the client manager gets the chance to rehearse their own role in the needs review meeting, while someone else plays the client. These mock needs reviews help to increase confidence and enhance your ability to focus the discussion when the meeting with the actual client occurs.

For many accountants entrenched in compliance work, the process of discovering a client's needs can be intimidating – especially when conducting your first few needs analysis meetings. You can neutralise any nervousness by first reaching out to clients with whom you have an established relationship. After all, you may as well start with whom you know well and practise on them to improve your disposition and gain experience.

Issues to cover in needs review meetings include (among many other points):

- Business strengths and weaknesses
- Future goals
- Competition issues
- Risk management
- Succession planning
- Funding management
- Lifestyle issues

Once you've established your client's needs, you can submit a customised proposal to them outlining how your advice could make a difference in the future success of their business.

How do you go about discovering your client's specific strengths and weaknesses? While this might seem like a daunting task, we can map it out for you to make it as streamlined as possible. Based on Matt's firsthand experience with real-life clients who have succeeded using his business advisory model, he says needs analysis meetings have helped both him and his clients nut out their strengths and weaknesses and, in turn, how he could best help his clients succeed.

In one case, Matt sat down with a client to go over the business's cash flow and find out where they could tie up some loose ends. A silent partner spoke up and asked for a strategic plan to be outsourced to another company. Matt saw this as an opportunity to throw his hat into the ring and take on that task. By taking on this assignment, he showed his clients he cared about their success and wanted to ensure they were supported in taking the next step.

After checking in with his clients, Matt ascertained that one of their strengths was the urge to get away from domestic work and have more capacity to focus on their own specific clients' needs. They began working on the business's communication with their market, focusing on their reliability (another key strength), which allowed them to target a key player in their industry. Although domestic work was usually their bread and butter income-wise, they weren't showing success in their profit margins. By working with Matt to shift focus, they were able to create consistent cash flow, which allowed them to work with their own employees instead of outsourcing to contractors. This allowed them to manage their costs much better and harness their strengths while nurturing the strong relationships they'd made along the way.

Matt also worked with his clients to define their weaknesses, which proved to be within their cash flow and payroll. With Matt's guidance, his clients identified which tasks could be outsourced to a consultant to ensure their staff were being awarded correctly.

You should approach each client with a 'can-do' attitude and show that you have the time to really figure out what they can tweak to harness their strengths to benefit their cash flow. Don't overlook their weaknesses – they play a big part too. While it can be tricky to point out a client's weaknesses, doing so is as vitally important as identifying their strengths when it comes to restructuring their outlook and approach to benefit their business. You want to reach a point where your experience to guide and ability to find the rose and thorn in your clients' businesses is second nature.

PRACTISING PERSEVERANCE IS KEY TO LEARNING TO WORK WITH YOUR CLIENTS DELICATELY AND TRANSPARENTLY.

In another case, one of Matt's clients, a podiatry clinic, hadn't checked their pricing structure in a long time. Matt questioned this, trying to understand how they managed their prices. The owner said their clinic, being the largest in their regional area, was the leader in pricing, and they didn't want to be undercut by a cheaper option. However, in the past, when the clinic had raised its prices, the competition responded by raising their own.

Matt explained that the best way to remain at the top in their area was to be ahead of the curve, pushing the pricing dynamic boundaries with their competition. After examining their overheads and realising the cost of equipment had gone up, Matt saw an opportunity for the clinic to raise its prices. His clients were hesitant at first, but Matt reminded them that based on their own experience with the competition in this regional centre, the others would follow their lead.

GO FISH!

Mark encourages you to think of step two of the Enabler™ as a fishing trip. Put the bait on your line and be patient when working with your prospective clients.

You can't meet your client with too many preconceived notions; however, you should be organised enough to know your purpose when meeting with them. Mark's method is to be prepared with approximately five questions ready to go for your needs analysis meetings.

1. **Business strengths:** "What's the best thing that's happened in your business in the last twelve months?"
2. **Business weaknesses:** "If you could go back and change one thing to improve your business, what would that be?"
3. **Risks:** "If something happened to you, could the business continue?"
4. **Funding:** "Are you looking to borrow money? If so, how much, when, and what for?"
5. **Succession:** "How long can you keep doing this before you lose your mind?"

A great way to start is to ask your client, "What's the best thing that has happened in your business over the last three months, six months, twelve months?" From there, use those answers as a launching pad to delve a bit deeper to get a complete picture of your client's needs. Once you get into the nitty-gritty in this initial meeting, you can walk away with, as Mark says, "A little bit of gold you can nurture and mine and eventually develop." You can then put everything you learnt from the client into a needs analysis proposal, which you'll provide within 7 days of the meeting. It's important to show initiative in this step and also follow through. Your reliability and tenacity will be a huge asset in securing business advisory work.

PARMI OR PARMA?

It's best to meet up with your clients in a neutral setting. This could be over a coffee, or having a schnitty parmi (or parma as Matt calls it) down at your local pub. The casual setting will allow your client to feel comfortable in opening up to you about their business, which can sometimes be daunting, especially if the business is struggling. The best advice from Matt and Mark is to avoid a clinical office setting due to disruptions and interruptions that could hinder your 'fishing trip'.

The casual setting also allows you to discover your clients' weaknesses more easily. For many people, a sore spot can be hard to admit, so when discussing this topic, your line of questions should be designed to drop your clients' walls. Two questions Mark proposes are, "What's one thing you would love to be able to do again, if you could?" and, "What's one thing you wish you'd never done?"

The next step is to talk about risk, another tricky topic. The aim is to assess what would happen to the business without your client working in it. Could it continue, or would it fall apart? The answer tells you a lot about your client and their business. For example, their business may be too dependent on them, or their ability to relinquish control may need to be investigated. Their answer may tell you they're in desperate need of succession work and a succession plan.

One of Mark's clients was an office equipment manufacturer and retailer in Sydney. Mark had input the client's data into a software program called Optimist, later known as Prophet Optimiser, which caused him to go into their next meeting with a lot of preconceived ideas. While the program ostensibly showed the business's strengths and weaknesses, once Mark began chatting to the client, all of those pre-programmed notions went out the window. Upon meeting for a coffee, Mark learnt that his client's sales had gone up by 4.88

percent, but his profit had gone down. Mark asked him, "How could this be?" The client mentioned that he had hired a new employee to increase sales and allow him to finally see his son play football after missing every Saturday game for the last 2 years. Work-life balance was a priority to him, so he made the financial sacrifice to allow him flexibility and coverage to prioritise other aspects of his life.

During the meeting, Mark went on to discuss his client's weaknesses, learning that the business's receivables had become uncontrollable. This revelation proved key in determining Mark's advisory steps to structure the business in a way that benefitted the client. A great tip – use these meetings to seek opportunity. If the client gives you an opening, harness it to determine which services you can offer to meet their needs. By unlocking the client's actual needs through connecting with him face to face, Mark learnt what software couldn't tell him and was able to provide informed guidance that enhanced the business.

Mark believes the way to your clients' hearts is to be solution-focused. When your client has developed enough trust with you to divulge their business concerns, it helps to try and solve the problem with them, not necessarily for them. When one problem is fixed, it's your job, with a solution-focused attitude, to delve deeper to fine-tune any other issues.

Another top tip is to ask your client open-ended questions, treating the meeting as if you're panning for gold. Closed questions often get closed answers and provide little opportunity to discover the gold you're looking for. You want to engage your client and get them talking about where they see themselves in 5 years' time to determine how you can best advise them to implement real strategies to maximise their profitability and productivity, and eventually allow them a better work-life balance.

This, however, isn't an exercise in note taking or ticking off a checklist. Instead, it's an exercise in client engagement. The client shouldn't be staring at the top of your head as you take notes. If you do need notes, especially as you fine-tune your advisory work, take a member of your staff with you to do the writing.

IF YOU WALK AWAY FROM YOUR MEETING WITH EVEN A SLIVER OF PRECIOUS GOLD, IT'S MORE THAN WHAT YOU STARTED WITH WHEN YOU WALKED IN. ULTIMATELY, YOUR SKILLS IN CLIENT ENGAGEMENT WILL OPEN UP MORE OPPORTUNITIES TO ASSIST YOUR CLIENTS AND EXPAND YOUR BUSINESS' SERVICES.

In his 40-year career, Mark has conducted over 4,000 client needs analysis meetings, and he encourages you to go in with zero expectations. The most valuable moments with your clients are usually the most unexpected. Even though you may not have all the answers, any information your clients can provide becomes the invaluable building blocks of your strategies once you learn to pivot. Pivoting, however, based on new information takes practice, and any fears you may have about not being able to shoulder unpredictability will slowly dissolve once you gain experience.

Watch the video:

The Client Needs "Fishing Trip" –
Five Questions Every Advisor Should Ask

LET ME GET BACK TO YOU ...

Matt emphasises that it really is okay to not know the answer to every question or query your client has. If you need to get back to them, "I don't know, but I'll find out for you" is a perfectly acceptable response. You might not have all the information you need right off the bat, but don't let that deter you. Instead, show your client you're willing and able to seek accurate answers.

The initial meeting is all about connecting with your client and working with them to find ways to improve their business. You won't be the salve for every issue. Matt encourages you to be a connector – someone who can introduce or link together services for your clients so they feel supported by you. Matt had a client with 24,000 Instagram followers, but for reasons unbeknownst to the client, he couldn't convert the online following into real life sales. Matt didn't offer a service that covered this issue, so he connected his client with a specialist, and now the business is booming. From there on out, Matt's client knew he could reach out to him for advice, and all it took was one email to find a solution. A simple action can create a closer bond with your client, letting them know they can rely on you and trust your services.

Mark knows all too well how important it is to create

a closer bond with your clients. Regarding business advisory, one question comes up frequently: How do you engage the client to meet with you? Mark explains that you start by calling your client and asking to meet for coffee using the 'reasonable person test', which assumes your client will have a reasonable response to the request, usually asking, "What for?"

From here, you can point out a strength and/or weakness associated with their business. For example, you may say, "I'm really concerned that your business is leaking cash, and I want to see how we can put a stop to it."

Naturally, the client may ask, "What's it going to cost me?"

Your answer – "It won't cost you anything, let's just meet up for a chat." Mark emphasises inviting your client to engage – that's all it takes.

"THERE REALLY IS NO MAGIC FORMULA, BUT RATHER IT'S ABOUT BEING INQUISITIVE, ASKING OPEN-ENDED QUESTIONS, LISTENING ACTIVELY, AND WANTING TO HELP YOUR CLIENT SUCCEED."

YOU SWOT, MATE?

Running a basic SWOT (strengths, weaknesses, opportunities, threats) analysis is a simple way to get your client thinking about their business. Here are some example questions you could ask based on Mark's and Matt's advice:

STRENGTH

- WHAT WOULD YOU SAY IS THE HIGHEST ACHIEVING SERVICE YOUR BUSINESS OFFERS?
- WHAT ARE YOU MOST PROUD OF ACCOMPLISHING IN THE LAST 12 MONTHS?
- WHICH SERVICE BRINGS IN THE HIGHEST CASHFLOW?
- WHAT IS ONE THING YOU'VE DONE THAT YOU'VE LOVED AND WOULD DO AGAIN?

WEAKNESS

- WHERE DO YOU SEE IMPROVEMENTS BEING MADE IN YOU BUSINESS?
- WHAT IS ONE THING YOU WISH THAT YOU NEVER DID?
- FROM YOUR OWN EXPERIENCE, WHAT DO YOU WANT OUT OF YOUR BUSINESS IN THE NEXT 12 MONTHS?

OPPORTUNITIES

- IS THERE A SERVICE IN YOUR INDUSTRY THAT YOU COULD OFFER THAT YOUR COMPETITION DOES NOT?
- HOW CAN WE PACKAGE YOUR PRICING TO BE UP TO DATE WITH INDUSTRY STANDARDS?
- WHO CAN WE PUT YOU IN TOUCH WITH TO IMPROVE MARKETING OPPORTUNITIES?

THREATS

- WHAT WOULD HAPPEN TO THE BUSINESS IF SOMETHING HAPPENED TO YOU?
- COULD THE BUSINESS CONTINUE WITHOUT YOU?
- IS YOUR BUSINESS UP TO DATE WITH MARKET TRENDS, TECHNOLOGY SYSTEMS AND STAFF TRAINING?

When Matt conducted an analysis with one of his clients, an electrical company, he found that the electrician was invoicing his clients at the end of the month rather than at the end of the completed job. It was a tradition handed down from the man's father decades earlier and hadn't been assessed since its inception. The business' strengths were their loyal customer base and solid history in the community, and customers would pay their invoices promptly. However, by invoicing once per month, the client was restricting his cash flow – a clear weakness. The small change of switching invoicing timelines streamlined his cash flow, and his business became better managed all around.

TIP FOR NEW PLAYERS: ASK THE RIGHT QUESTIONS

Getting into the rhythm of asking the right questions is critical to success as a business advisory firm. These types of questions will help elicit your clients' needs:

- How's business?
- How do you feel about the role you play in your business?

- What trends are you seeing in your business this year versus last year?
- How are you performing against budget or expectations this year?
- What has been the greatest success you've had in your business in the last 12 months?
- If you had the chance to make key decisions over the last 12 months again, what would they be?
- Are you dispensable? Have you ever been able to take 4 weeks leave?
- Have you ever thought about selling the business or retiring? What kind of time scale are you looking at?
- Are you comfortable that your assets and family are protected?
- What about your business keeps you awake at night?

Your responses to your client's answers can stimulate discussion and open their mind to the possibility of engaging with you further. Great responses include:

1. Our focus is to help you achieve your life goals by …

2. Creating a business that's easily saleable when the time comes

3. Making you financially independent so you have funds for holidays, your kids' education, and your retirement

4. Protecting your family's income and assets

5. Helping you plan for and manage business succession and estate matters

From there, you can scope out the possibilities and write a proposal that really sells your services.

Mark has designed a handy guide entitled '10 by 10 Needs Review' with 100 open-ended questions you can use when meeting with your client and writing up your needs analysis report. Their comprehensive list is excellent to have on hand, as the questions allow you to get a deeper insight into your client's mindset (find out more in the appendix at the back of the book!). Your client's needs are divided into ten categories, each with ten questions, to help you delve into the nitty-gritty and get stuck into how you can assist your client to succeed.

Here are some examples you can use while working through step two of the Enabler™ process (unlock your clients' needs):

1. **Business Profitability Improvement**
   What has been the greatest success you've had in your business over the past 12 months?

2. **Business Conditions**
   Describe the difference between your business and your competitors' businesses. What are they doing better than you? What are you doing better than them?

3. **Marketing**
   How do you feel about using social media to market your business? If you are using it, how could you improve the impact of your social media activity?

4. **Technology and Process**
   How has technology change been impacting your business? How should you be responding to these changes?

5. **Human Resources**
   How do you feel the management of your employees might be improved?

6. **Finance**

   Will any existing funding need to be
   rolled over in the next 12 to 18 months?
   What plans do you have in place to
   manage this?

7. **Risk Management**

   What are your three biggest business
   risks, and how do you plan to
   manage them?

8. **Succession Planning**

   Do you want to sell your business? If so,
   how much do you think the business is
   worth now?

9. **Retirement**

   Have you considered when you're going
   to retire? If so, when do you think
   that may be?

10. **Family/Personal**

    What are the obstacles making it hard
    for you to achieve your goals?

When you ask the right questions, you get the right answers, leading to a better understanding of how to best help your clients succeed. Once you gain that understanding, the next step is to prove the value of the services you're offering.

10 by 10 Needs Review

STEP 3

CREATE A DISTURBANCE IN YOUR CLIENTS' MINDS

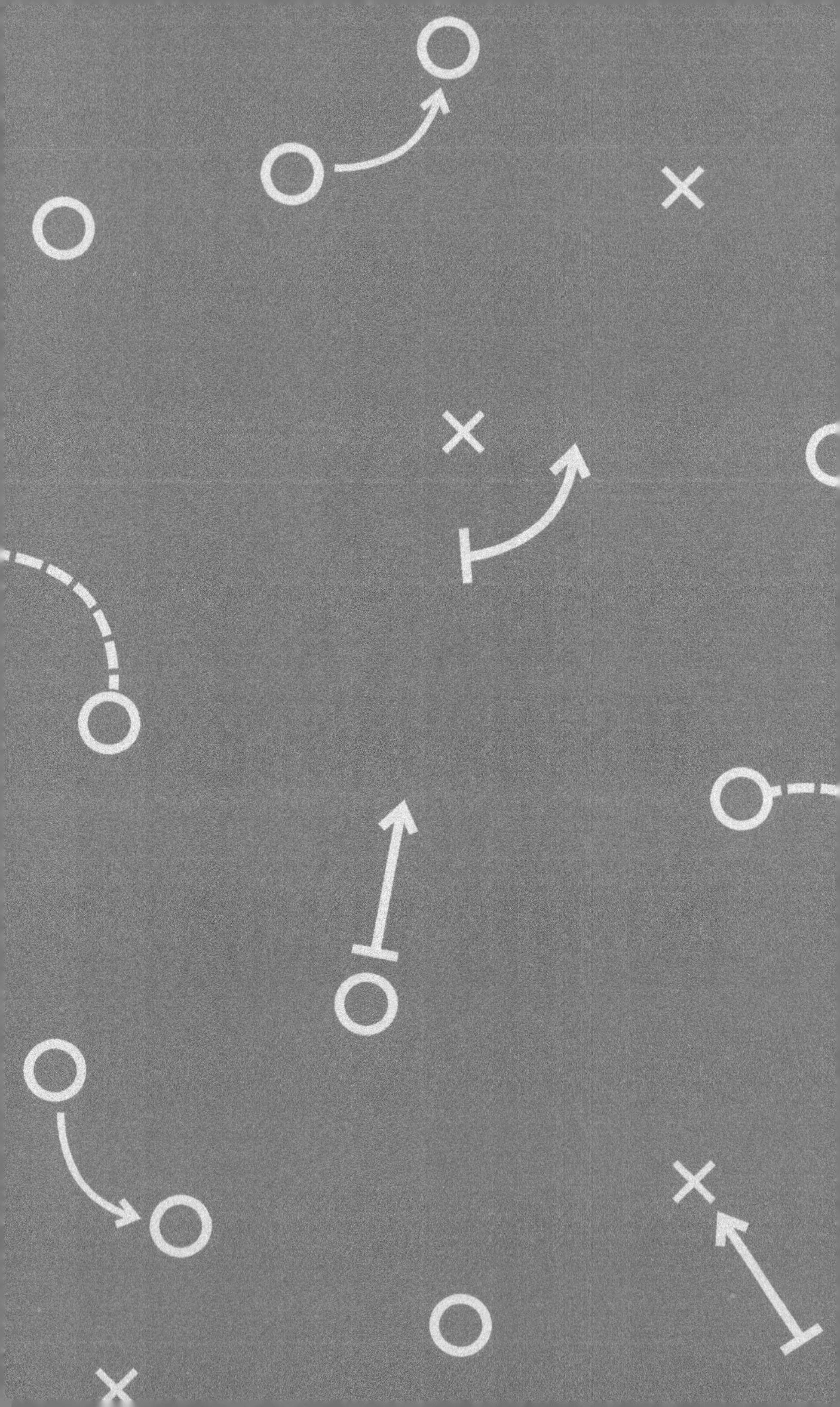

Being able to quickly demonstrate the value and validity of your advisory services to your clients is critical to success. It all begins with challenging your own set of routines.

You and your clients are likely in a routine that feels safe, predictable even. However, your clients will have personal goals and pressures, and taking the time to understand your clients from a more personal perspective allows you to delve into where you can provide them the most value.

Step three is about unlocking not only your mind but also your clients' minds and getting them excited and interested in improving their businesses.

After building a successful compliance-based division of his practice, Matt was faced with a life-changing event – the need for major surgery at the age of 36 and a lengthy recovery, which would take him away from the practice. In preparation, he transitioned his compliance work to other team members so he could have 3 months to recover from the operation.

On his return and with a blank slate, Matt was challenged by his partners and board to create a business advisory division. With an empty diary and a new focus, he was free to engage clients in meaningful discussions about their business and life goals, the problems they were facing, and how he could help. This was the foundation for a successful transition to business advisory. In reality, the transition was simple and only required a break in routine and a small but dedicated amount of time each week to discuss more than just tax with clients. So, how will you make the same simple transition?

LOOKING TOWARDS TOMORROW

In many instances, providing your client with a business value indication can help initiate an engagement. How do you do this? If you're an accountant, you may have conducted a business valuation in the past. They're generally used for partnership disputes, family law settlements, or to buy or sell a business. To break it down, a business valuation is a discussion between an accountant and their client that details how much their business is currently worth, how valuable their business will be in the future, and how to bridge the gap between today and tomorrow.

Mark knows that the best way to create a disturbance in your client's mind is to meet with them and demonstrate the hard value of advisory services to their business. He enters such meetings with one succession question: "How long can you keep doing this before you negatively impact your mental wellbeing?" Or, in his words, "… before you go nuts!"

One of his clients couldn't imagine himself still working in his own business in 5 years. Mark saw this as an opportunity to harness his skills to set up a 5-year plan to alleviate his client's worries. He asked his client, "What do you want this business to be worth in five years' time so you can walk away and say, 'I've received a really good return on that investment'?" His client, although fully stocked with investment properties, share portfolios, managed funds, and bank accounts, hadn't thought of his business as an investment in itself. Mark was able to create a disturbance in his client's thinking, pivoting how the client thought of his business and, in turn, Mark's offerings as a business advisor.

The next step was to engage with his client regarding their 5-year plan. What was their EBIT (earnings before interest and tax) goal? His client wanted to triple his EBIT before the 5 years were up, increasing it to $1.5 million. Mark asked him, "What's your business worth today?"

His client quipped, "Well, you're the accountant, why don't you tell me?" Mark saw this as an opportunity to determine the value of the business today and how he could increase that value tomorrow. The key was to work out the gap and then work on the strategy to close that gap over the coming years. You don't present your client with a 50-page document, but rather sit down with them and have a visual discussion around achieving their goals.

Mark uses an approach that works wonders for his advisory business. He asks his clients to work with him quarterly, running board of advice meetings, to improve their profitability, strengthen their cash flow, and de-risk their businesses. The key is to eliminate the risk factors. For example, one of his client's accounts receivable had extended by roughly 40 days over the last 2 years, causing a cash flow leak – a huge risk. By reducing the number of days they were receiving payment, they made the business less risk-prone. The aim is to get the client to look forward and dream about what tomorrow can bring.

THE BUSINESS VALUE
INDICATION MODEL
IS ALL ABOUT SEEING
HOW YOU CAN MAKE
A CLIENT'S BUSINESS
MORE VALUABLE
THAN IT IS TODAY. IT'S
ABOUT HARNESSING
TOMORROW AND
LOOKING TO CREATE
HIGHER VALUE IN
THE FUTURE.

Why? Because many SME owners want to know how much their investments are worth, and often business value indications turn out to be below their expectations. The gap between expectation and reality creates an incentive for them to implement the changes necessary to increase their business value, and consequently they become more likely to pay for your business advice.

Alternatively, if your client is looking for or expecting to need finance for their business soon, conducting a lending pre-assessment can help them understand whether they're likely to be able to access funding from lenders. Again, if their expectations aren't aligned with the likely outcome of their loan application, they may not be compelled to make necessary changes.

Using scenario-planning software that allows you to address key lending covenants (EBITDA [earnings before interest, taxes, depreciation, and amortisation], interest cover, debt service cover, liquidity, gearing and capital adequacy) can help you work with your clients to overcome their funding gaps.

INTRODUCING PROPHET GAP

Mark and Matt have developed an incredibly useful, innovative, and easy-to-use software platform designed to make the process a breeze for both you and your clients. Prophet Gap (prophetgap.com) makes onboarding your clients into additional advisory services easier and more engaging than ever. It's designed to save you time and money while growing your fee base and winning more work. If you're having a hard time engaging your business clients with advisory work and creating a disturbance in their minds, Prophet Gap allows you to show off the magic in your arsenal and gain insights into their thoughts about their businesses.

So how does Prophet Gap work? Firstly, you send your client a private link from your app, and they'll answer a series of AI-powered questions. From there, you'll receive their answers so you can plan how to help them. The platform combines data to provide insight into your client's needs alongside their hopes and goals for tomorrow. Not only that, but it also works as a training model, allowing you to easily train staff within your firm to onboard clients into advisory services. Essentially, Prophet Gap is an online tool for starting the conversation with your clients and retaining their business for longer. Want to see the platform in action?

Go to prophetgap.com to book a demonstration

WHEN TOMORROW EQUALS RETIREMENT

Other disturbances to create in your clients' minds may include discussing their financial preparedness for retirement or the expenses of their kids' education. Matt emphasises how important it is to discuss retirement and succession with your clients. He has advised many clients who are closer to becoming one of Australia's lucky grey nomads just how important it is, before retirement, to nurture and train those who are set to take over their roles.

Through utilising business advisory, you can impart your knowledge gained from experience with a wide range of clientele and advise your clients how to transition out of their businesses successfully. Matt recommends advising your clients on how to engage management training or even improve their staff's soft skills to make the handover easier. You can create a disturbance in a checked-out client's mind by showing them how to check in on their successor and do everything to ensure their business isn't set up to failure due to a lack of training. In all instances, your objective is to demonstrate that you can help them bridge the gap between where they are now and where they want to be in the future.

Think of it this way. What would you say if you were talking to a client about your business advisory services and they asked you, "What's in it for me?" You can use that question to pan for gold and work with them to show how your services are exactly what they need to set themselves up for the future.

In our experience, the most appealing answer is usually, "I'll help you make your business worth more!"

Matt was discussing with a client his ideal timeframe for retirement and what he believed he needed to retire. The client indicated that he wanted to retire in 5 to 7 years, selling his business for $5 million. He assumed it wasn't something worth worrying about for 3 or so years. Matt recommended doing a value analysis to be sure the business was close to the mark. The analysis highlighted that, at best, the business would achieve a sale of $3 million. Additionally, because the business was essentially a one-man-band operation, Matt advised the client that he would potentially have to work in the business for 2 years to satisfy the vendor and ensure the full goal purchase price was achieved.

Ultimately, Matt highlighted several deficiencies:

1. The client had 3 years to build the business to the sale value of $4 million.
2. The client had to sell the business in 4 to 5 years' time to be retired by 7 years, while ensuring the handover and earn outs were achieved.
3. The majority of the business was run based on the business owner's undocumented knowledge, meaning there were no documented processes in place to ensure a successful handover to the purchaser.

These discoveries led to quarterly meetings to ensure all problems were resolved and the business was ready for its eventual sale.

TIP FOR NEW PLAYERS – GET THE RIGHT TOOLS FOR THE JOB

Creating a disturbance in your clients' minds is most effective when you have software at your disposal to quickly calculate value and perform 'what-if' scenarios. With the right software on hand, you'll be well equipped to analyse your clients' business performance in the next stage of the Enabler™ process.

Tools we would never be without in a business advisory firm include:

1. Tools to identify what's important to the client (Prophet Gap for example).

2. Administrative tools that manage opportunities, actions, outcomes, and projects – in other words, a customer relationship management (CRM) solution.

3. Budgeting and cash flow solutions that integrate with the clients accounting systems. The features you need may already be built into the software you're currently paying for!

4. Business valuation indication software.

5. Scenario-planning software that runs 'what-if' scenarios and displays the 'power of one' (which we'll discuss in the next chapter).

Check the appendix at the back of the book for our software recommendations for each category.

Now that you understand the importance of creating a disturbance in your clients' minds, it's time to talk more analysis, specifically analysing your clients' financial performance.

STEP 4

ANALYSE YOUR CLIENTS' FINANCIAL PERFORMANCE

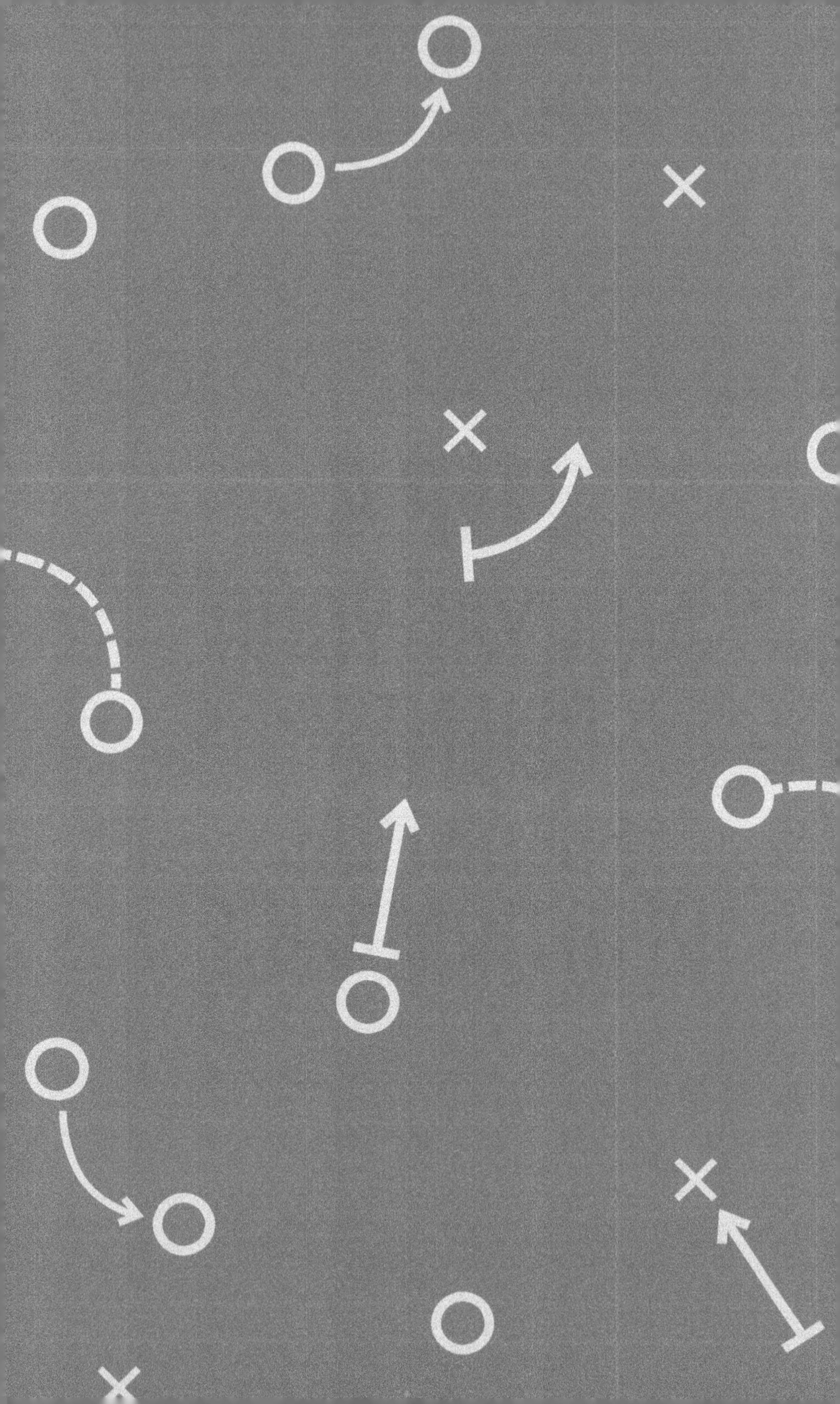

The previous step of the Enabler™ process is a historical review: What has happened in the business so far? Step four is all about how you can help your clients by looking into the future for them. It's time to get out your crystal ball and analyse your clients' financial performance.

Mark sees the merit in conducting a 'what-if analysis'. For example, determining the impact decisions will have on a client's business before they make them. Mark's business advisory mantra is, "How would you like to see the financial impact of key business decisions before you make them?" A large number of clients tend to go off on their own and make decisions that negatively impact them down the line, and their advisor or accountant struggles to put out the fire already sparked.

"THE WHOLE POINT OF ADVISORY ISN'T TO LOOK INTO THE PAST, BUT RATHER TO LOOK FORWARD AND MAKE DECISIONS KNOWING THEY'RE THE RIGHT ONES."

You're asking your clients, "Now that we're working together, what levers do we need to pull, and how hard, in order to reach your goals?" When looking into the future, we have the ability to envision and mould the outcomes we want to achieve. As Matt says, "It's prevention, rather than a cure." He knows it's best to guide clients to make decisions rather than mistakes. He has a two-step approach to achieving this:

1. Track the outcome your client wants to achieve and keep their decisions on the right path.
2. As Kenny Rogers says, "know when to fold 'em" and be prepared to cease moving forward when you realise the plan isn't going as intended. If you do a what-if analysis, you can review it in real time and know when it's time to throw in the towel.

Watch the video:
The Decision-Making Insight Your
Clients Have Been Waiting For

THE POWER OF ONE

Let's now dive into some 'what-if' scenarios. Mark uses the 'power of one' model to help guide his clients' decisions. For example, if you increase the pricing of your products by 1 percent, how will this benefit the business? If you collect your client payments 1 day earlier, what will the outcome be? If you turn over your stock or inventory 1 day sooner, how will it impact the business? In the purest sense, this is the power of one. What will happen if you increase or decrease something by one step, one percent, or one positive moment?

There's a common misconception in the business advisory sphere that increasing a business's prices means losing customers. However, businesses that don't increase their prices at the right times fail to stay competitive. If you advise your client to increase their prices by 5 percent and they lose 5 percent of their customers, you've essentially made the same amount of money. This is what's known as a 'goal seek' where you seek to understand the benefits of a decision before it's made. When analysing a client's financial performance, it's imperative to delve into the positives, neutrals, and negatives of all potential decisions.

MARK'S AND MATT'S REAL-LIFE EXPERIENCES

Matt's client had excessive stock in their warehouse, stating that their sales had plummeted. Matt asked if they were offering discounts to potential and past customers to help move the stock. The client hadn't considered this approach, so Matt encouraged them to use old stock and sell it at wholesale pricing so they could at least break even on product that had been sitting there for a while. Essentially, he gave the client a new perspective and got money coming through the door. The best way to engage a client is to get in the trenches with them. Take a walk around their warehouse, go with them to see a potential commercial space, see what their day to day looks like, and you'll find ways to implement your advisory services.

Mark remembers a client who had come to meet with him to discuss a factory he had just purchased due to his current factory having issues with rent, landlords, and the quality of the facilities. Because Mark already had the business's data saved in the software he was using to detail the client's goals, he understood the situation and realised the client had made a mistake. Mark pondered how to address this with his client, finally saying, "Mate, you're not thinking about this properly. Why didn't you come to me first to talk it out?"

His client responded, "I didn't even know you offered that service." Mark felt a massive kick to his ego that day. How can a client know you can help them if you never tell them? From that day on, Mark was determined to let all of his clients know how he could help their businesses.

Knowing he was unable to change what had already happened, Mark moved to plan B. He encouraged his client to cut the new factory in half and sublease one half to another business. Although his client had to work in a smaller setting until, financially, he could take on the mortgage of the entire factory, Mark's knowledge helped turn a potential blunder into a long-term win.

Matt analysed the financial statements of one client and realised they were paying $200,000 to a subcontractor to do a particular job. When Matt priced up the purchase of the required machinery and hiring someone for the role full time, it came to $150,000. He took this information to his client and advised him to cease working with a subcontractor, as hiring a team member would not only cost less but also allow him to train them to work within the bounds of his business model. Additionally, on days when the staff member wasn't needed, the business could send them to help someone else in their industry, strengthening relationships and bringing in more work. Matt knows the importance of assessing a client's financial strengths and weaknesses and fine-tuning them to benefit their business.

Mark and Matt want you to know that the best way to engage clients is to listen, ask open-ended questions, be inquisitive, and be direct. You have the answers your clients need, and you can strategically follow up with them to deliver the best results. You don't need to follow a script or a set of rules – each client will need something different. If you don't ask questions, you don't know what your clients need, and you can't turn their answers into a service.

TO BE STRONG, YOU MUST BE ABLE TO SEE WEAKNESS

Diving headfirst into your client's strengths and weaknesses is a pivotal moment when moving through step four of the Enabler™ process, just as much as it is in step two. You need to gain the clarity to see what they're doing right and wrong, and voice that in a professional yet clear manner. Once you hit that level of transparency with your client, offering your services becomes easier and more lucrative.

Matt knows that a great way to discover a client's strengths and weaknesses is by talking to them one on one, asking questions like:

- "Are you taking enough holidays?"
- "Are you making the money you would make, or more, if you were a salaried employee?"

Asking these types of questions is a great way to get your client thinking while you look at the numbers and highlight discoveries to support your discussion. You may find that your client's sales have dropped, but their gross profit margin is up, meaning they made more money for doing less work that year. Alternatively, you may find that your client's sales are up, but so is the cost of goods sold, therefore resulting in a loss. This presents an opportunity for you and your client to explore the issue further.

It may not always be about sales every single time. Your client's work-life balance is just as much of a priority. Matt has a client who came to him wanting to be able to get to school pick-up on time after finding themselves frequently staying late at work. Matt asked him to do a benchmark and, from this, was able to map out a way for his client to extend their quality time with their kids. Four years later, Matt's still conducting monthly meetings with them to assess how the business is feeding their lifestyle and allowing them to find just as much success in their home life as their working life.

FIND IT, FIX IT, FIX IT FAST

Mark has coined a term called the three Fs: find it, fix it, and fix it fast. This notion applies when you and your client have discovered their weaknesses and, in serious scenarios, your client is 'in the red' and needs your help to move to the 'green'.

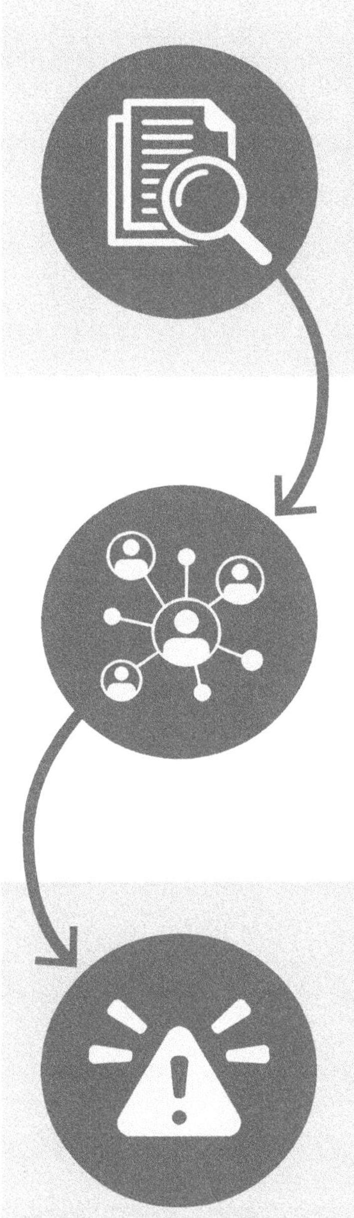

FIND IT:
FIND OUT FROM THE CLIENT THE ISSUE THAT NEEDS TO BE REMEDIED: UNLOCK THE CLIENTS NEEDS, ASK YOUR CLIENT TO USE PROPHET GAP, TALK TO THEM ONE ON ONE ASKING SERIES OF QUESTIONS TO DIVE INTO THE ISSUE, AND FINALLY ANALYSE THE NUMBERS.

FIX IT:
DEPENDING ON THE PROBLEM, YOU CAN REACH OUT TO YOUR NETWORK TO PAIR YOUR CLIENT WITH THE SPECIALIST THEY NEED.

FIX IT FAST!:
GET IT DONE ASAP!

Scenario-planning software like Cash Flow Story that allows you to develop 'what-if' scenarios and 'power of one' projection is ideal for this purpose. It enables you to show your clients the financial impact of various business decisions before they make them, analyse their strengths and determine how to make them stronger, and find any weaknesses and implement fast fixes to convert them into strengths.

While many firms invest in this type of software, in our experience, fewer than 20 percent use it to its full potential. Effective utilisation of scenario-planning software really can establish you as a true expert in your clients' eyes. Just showing them the effects that small changes can have on their profitability and cash flow can quickly have them viewing you as a genius! Scenario-planning software also helps you to easily develop plans, budgets, and KPIs for your clients.

So, while it's not essential to have everyone in the firm become an expert in using scenario-planning software, it's well worth investing the time and money to train someone on your team to understand the software inside and out. Aside from the heavy lifting that person can do behind the scenes, it's great to be able to bring the team software guru along to meetings to run the program while you focus on your clients and the outcomes you can help them achieve.

SCENARIO-PLANNING SOFTWARE BREAKDOWN

Combined with your expertise, scenario-planning software helps show your clients the likely outcomes of important decisions such as:

- Whether to buy or sell a business, or participate in a merger or takeover
- If and when to make capital purchases, and how to fund them
- Whether to rent or buy new premises – and when
- Whether it's better for them to hire a new employee, or outsource
- When to declare dividends, launch new products, or change pricing
- When and how to enter or develop overseas markets, or tender for government contracts

Scenario-planning software also gives you the tools to assist your clients in:

- Developing business plans, budgets, and cash flow projections
- Setting their sales targets
- Managing their accounts receivable, payable, WIP (work in progress), and inventory
- Planning for succession, tax management, and wealth creation

Note: If you've invested in scenario-planning software and you're yet to fully come to grips with it, please contact us to discuss available solutions. We'd be delighted to help you maximise your return on investment.

Step four of the Enabler™ is when the proverbial rubber hits the road. It's when you can take action and really start to work with your clients to see tangible results. This is the moment when your delivery of advisory services begins to take form. The previous steps are about developing relationships, analysing needs, and creating a disturbance, and now you can finally take practical action. The next step is to ensure your clients implement your advice.

STEP 5

ENSURE YOUR CLIENTS IMPLEMENT ACTION

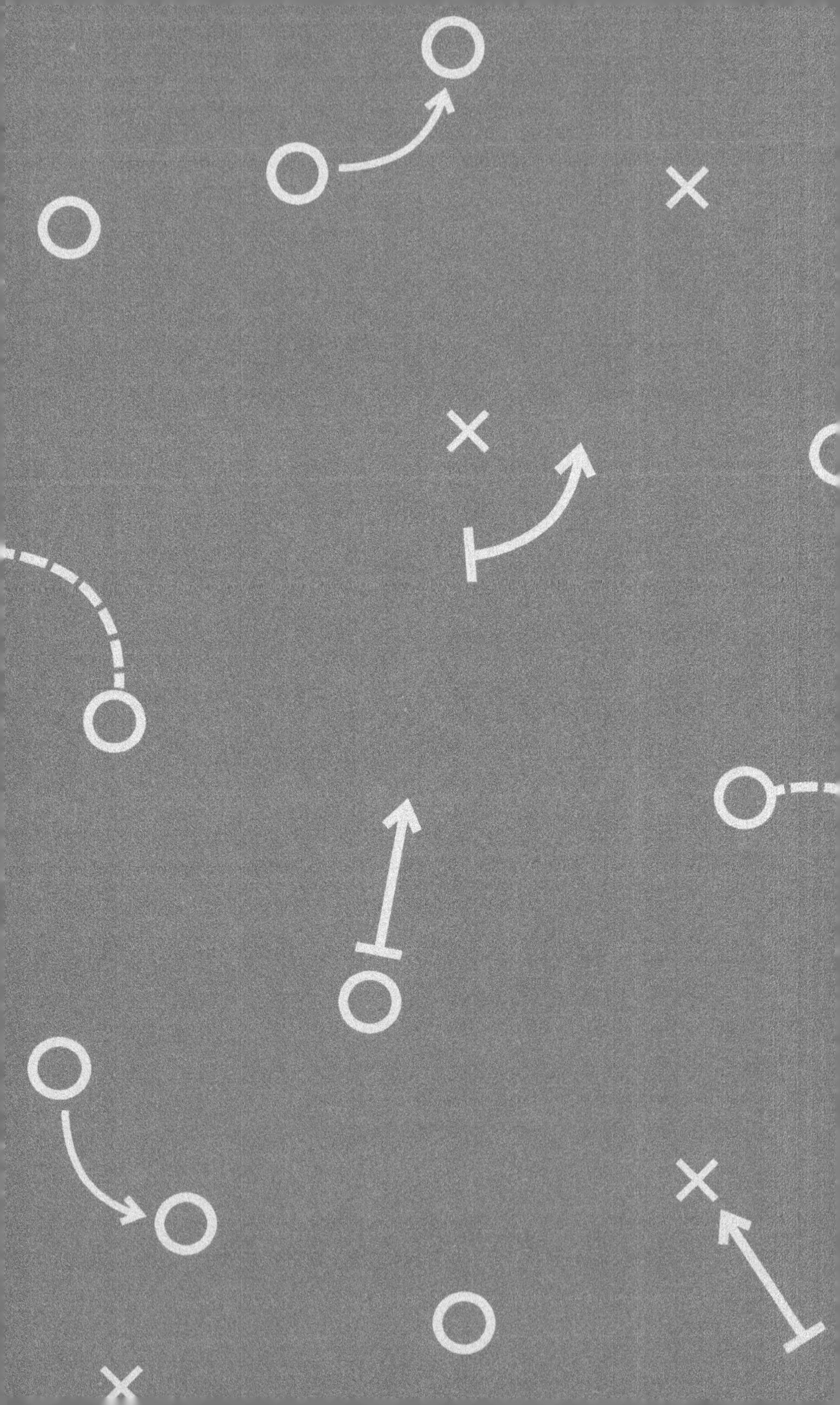

Like it or not, you're competing for business advisory work with coaches and other advisers who have less financial expertise than you and are often not as qualified to successfully influence your clients' financial future.

At the start of Mark's teaching career, he had to complete a degree in education, and one of the first set of principles taught to him were the four steps of education.

1. You tell the student: advise your client on how best to improve their business practices based on their financial performance and any future goals.
2. You show the student: show your client how to get there, whether that be by introducing them to contacts or encouraging them to reassess their business model.
3. You let the student do it: client uses tools you've provided to put your advice into practice.
4. You review it: catch up with your client to see how their business is going and determine if your advice should be expanded or amended.

HOWDY, PARTNER!

Matt knows the importance of explaining to your client that your relationship is a partnership. You respect that they know their industry inside and out, and you're bringing a broader business knowledge to the table. From there, you can ensure your client is implementing action by working together to achieve desired outcomes or brainstorm new ideas for their business. The next step is to remind your client that it's their business. They'll have to do the day-to-day work to get their business to where they want it to go. Finally, you should reassure your client that your business advisory work has been successful with other clients and it's all about making positive change.

Mark's best advice is to not sit back and presume the client is going to do what you advised just because you said so. You've got to follow up with them consistently to ensure your strategies aren't falling by the wayside. You can't have accountability without a plan. Without a plan, without structure, there's no bar set for your clients. One such plan is checking in with them every couple of weeks to ensure they're on the right path. It may only be for a few minutes, but showing interest in your clients' businesses will develop your partnerships even further while holding them accountable. Mark wants you to get in there and get your hands dirty!

DON'T BE AFRAID TO APPROACH YOUR CLIENTS ON A GRASSROOTS LEVEL AND SHOW THEM YOU'RE PREPARED TO DO THE WORK.

If you ever find yourself with a client who seems resistant to your business advice, Mark recommends pivoting to plan B, which involves asking them to meet face to face with both you and someone who can help with their specific issue. Perhaps the client has customers owing on their invoices. In this case, you could bring a debt collector along to show the client you're prepared and ready to solve their issues. The main message is to never sit on your hands. Instead, be proactive, be personal, and remember – this is a partnership.

When it comes to checking in with clients, it's critical to get them to see the positive outcomes of your partnership. As Matt explains, they must understand the importance of taking action. To illustrate that importance, you can present an example that has worked in the past with other clients and outline the steps to replicate that success. For example, if you have a client who continually finds themselves chasing invoices, you may advise the following: "The faster you can get the invoice raised and paid, the longer the money sits in your bank account and not in your customer's. You can't eat or pay a mortgage with work in progress or debtors. Don't let your customer use you as a credit union."

One of Matt's clients is the best he's ever seen at

collecting debts. They're one of the nicest and friendliest people on the planet. However, if you're even 1 day overdue, expect to speak to them on the phone every day until the invoice is paid. No aggression, no threats — you simply get sick of their name popping up on your phone. So what do you do? You pay the invoice! Calling is key, as email can simply be deleted.

Mark and Matt use tried and tested systems and strategies to hold clients accountable and help them stick to their goals. As a business advisor, you need to adopt some of those strategies, continually bringing your clients' attention back to their wants and needs, the gap between where they are now and where they want to be, and their strategy for bridging that gap.

Matt recommends reminding your clients that sometimes things won't go as planned. In fact, more often than not, your clients' plans won't pan out exactly as they want. This is why it's imperative to track and measure your actions to see if they're achieving the desired result, a negative result, or no result at all. There's no point in making changes if you're unable to monitor and report on the impact.

Let your client know you're there to help them complete any tasks. If your client promises to follow through on a task by the next meeting and they fail to do so, don't be afraid to let them know that this isn't good enough. In a partnership, being candid is often the hardest but most impactful way to communicate, and holding your clients accountable produces the best results.

Reassure your clients that it's okay to challenge you. You may present ideas that have worked for previous clients in the same situation but may not be ideal for others. Each business is different, and if a client has knowledge of a specific industry, allow and encourage them to voice it to you.

Be inquisitive, ask questions, and be sure to listen. If you don't receive a completely honest answer from your client, be quiet. People dislike awkward silences, and they'll talk about anything and everything to fill the space. These moments can be golden opportunities to insert your business advisory expertise and sell your services.

Mark does one thing with every single one of his business advisory clients: he holds a quarterly board of advice meeting where he examines their progress and holds them accountable. What actions have they taken since the last quarterly meeting? Why have they or haven't they completed what they set out to do? What do they need to help them achieve their short-term and long-term goals in the future?

It's up to you to be a financial and business coach and diarise regular emails and phone calls to see how your clients are progressing – or to get your client service manager to call and ask them. Regular enthusiastic contact helps keep your clients accountable and on track.

Watch the video:

One Action a Week; How
Accountability Unlocks Client Results

REAL-LIFE ACCOUNTABILITY – TOP TIPS

Now for some of Matt's and Mark's top tips for applying an accountability strategy to your real work and clients:

- Schedule phone calls outside of your usual meeting times just to see how things are going. Keep it casual and spur-of-the-moment so you can receive your clients' feedback in the most organic way. Ask questions like: How are things going? What's something you've done to implement the plan? What has been a roadblock for you? Once you have this information, it'll be a lot easier to work with them to move forward.

- Call your client out if they haven't been doing the work. You can keep things professional and friendly; however, holding your client to account is important when enacting business advisory. Let them know they've wasted time and explain the adverse impacts. Be straightforward and real with your clients.

- If you see hesitancy within your client when you suggest an action, jump on that hesitation. You can use this moment to remind them you'll be following up with them to ensure they complete the task. Matt did this with his very own brother regarding a pricing increase.
- Mark likes to sit down with his clients and create a plan for the next 12 months. That plan could include a price increase, an adjustment to output, or staff changes and management. A clear plan helps keep clients accountable, as they can see exactly where they are in relation to their goals and where they need to be. It's also important to understand the

potential impact of any changes before making them.

- Remind your clients why they came to you in the first place. Show them the reasons they needed your help and how you helped them initially. This keeps your clients focused on their future and success.

- It's important to remind your clients they agreed to the plan. As an advisor, it's your job to identify what's going right or wrong and keep them on the right path. At the end of the day, your clients agreed to your services, and sometimes you may need to remind them of that fact.

- Focus on solutions. Your job is to provide answers and advice to your clients to ensure their goals are met while working with them to identify and solve any problems. If a client comes to you with an issue, your first thought should be how to fix it.

You can fancy yourself as a financial handyman of sorts. Can you fix it?

Yes you can!

PRACTISE WHAT YOU PREACH

As with other steps in the Enabler™ process, you'll be most effective at step five if you develop a system, in this case, for following up with your clients and stick to it. So how do you do this?

Initially, reach out using email and phone calls – one of each. As the famous idiom goes, "You can lead a horse to water, but you can't make him drink." Matt has changed this idiom to suit his experience in business advisory: "You can drown a horse in water, but not to make it drink." Because occasionally, when dealing with clients, this is how it feels. At this point, you can approach your client for an honest conversation and explain that they may not be in the correct headspace to continue. The issue here is if your client is unable or unwilling to do the work, they'll end up paying you and not getting any results.

You'll also need to be both patient and consistent. Despite your convictions, it's not uncommon for clients to take 6 or 12 months or more to start implementing all your suggestions. In our experience, it's not normally that they don't trust your recommendations, but that they might need time to get their head around the implications, feel comfortable making the investment, or free up the time to take action.

Candidly, Mark admits he's not a patient person in everyday life. However, he has respect for the person he's talking to and understands that, although he's tenacious, he has to exercise patience in order to achieve the desired outcome. You must treat your clients the way you would want to be treated. Listen to what they say – *really* listen. Don't just move to the next question on your checklist. Listen for what fills the silent moments too.

Through his experience in business advisory, Matt knows you may stumble upon mental blocks. If this situation arises, it's important to go back to your roots and practise what you preach. Hold the mirror up to yourself and ask if you're running the 'perfect' business or advising clients to do things you don't do yourself.

When Matt does his annual review of his ongoing engagements and decides to increase his pricing, if the client challenges him on this decision, he explains why it's necessary, reminding them that he's running his business efficiently and effectively, which is why the client engages him as a business advisor. Essentially, he practises what he preaches.

When advising your clients, you won't always have the knowledge to achieve the best outcomes. That's where step six comes in, where you draw on your contacts and network to solve client problems.

STEP 6

SERVICE ADDITIONAL CLIENT NEEDS

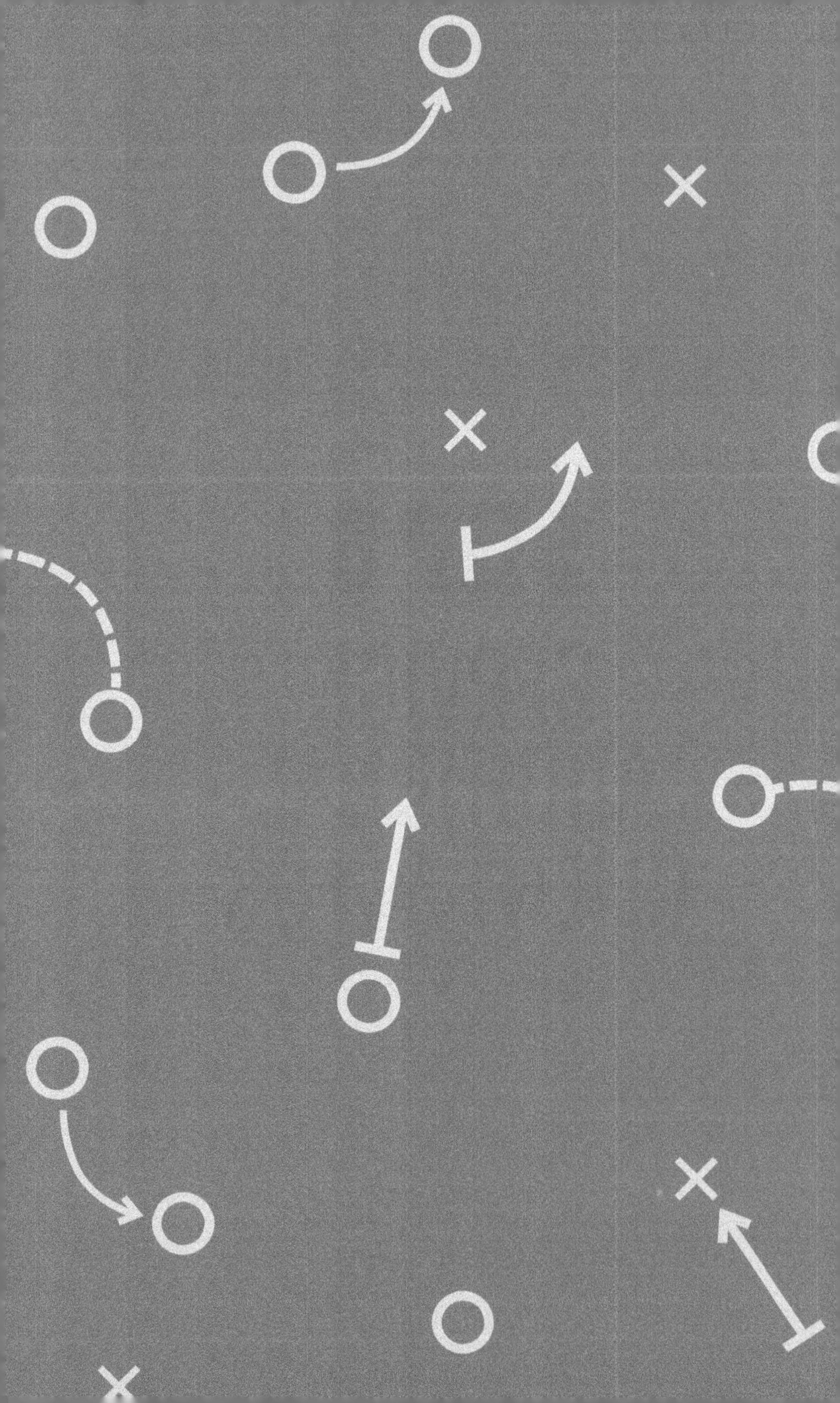

Budgets and cash flow targets should evolve into month-by-month action plans as a result of the financial analysis you performed for your client in step four of the Enabler™ process. In many cases, these actions alone can revolutionise the profitability of a small business. According to Matt, this is where the real nitty-gritty begins in terms of leaning into your advisory services. Budgets and cash flow are concepts that, as an accountant, you should be very comfortable with. At this point, however, it's time to stop resting upon straightforward financial metrics. So how do you forecast what's good and bad for you and your client? It's time to start digging.

Prophet Gap not only allows your clients to assess their own needs, wants, and goals, but it can also help you dig a little deeper into each facet. Questions that may pop up as you begin your dig include:

- What are you doing in terms of human resources?
- Do you have the right KPIs?
- Are your staff in the right roles?
- Are those staff working for the right salary?
- What else can I do for you?
- What do you need now that you know what you want?

- Who will be your successor?
- Who takes care of your estate?

Cash flow and budgets may help you through the first 2 to 3 initial meetings with your client, but in Matt's experience, you need to delve deeper to maintain your client's interest and prevent them from disengaging from your services. You don't want to get your client engaged, fired up, and paying for your service only to lose their business due to keeping your services superficial. However, as your relationship with your client develops, so too will their trust in you, your understanding of their business, and the amount of influence you have on its performance. Over time, you'll find opportunities to help your advisory clients with more and more of their business needs, above and beyond pure finance.

The key is to sit down with your clients and really find out what's causing them grief and how you can fine-tune their businesses using your advisory services.

Mark describes this portion of the Enabler™ program as the time to go 'above the line'. Any accounting work – that is, services you can provide yourself within your own accounting firm – is 'below the line'. 'Above the line' services are those you have to search for. While you can provide them, to do so, you need to search your databases and get in touch with your centres of influence. For example, reaching out to a HR specialist if your client needs help with their human resources department.

Matt has a client who came to him not knowing if he was paying his staff award rates for overtime correctly. Seeing this as an opportunity to help his client out, Matt let them know that this could potentially be a huge risk to their business. The next step was for Matt to introduce his client to his HR specialist who assessed the situation, showed them the ropes, and solved the issue within the week. Matt simply provided the information he had collated about his client to the specialist and let them take over from there.

Another client who's running a startup is paying Matt a monthly retainer. They had a great concept for their business and had reached out to a really big player in their industry. This big player was inspired by the client and wanted to take a chance on funding the startup with a $100,000 investment, but not without insurance papers drawn up. Matt's client called him in a panic, unsure of how to deal with the caveat. Although on the road delivering Christmas hampers to his clients, Matt rang his solicitor and had insurance paperwork drawn up before Christmas break, which meant his client was able to relax with their family and celebrate landing a huge investment! His client didn't have to think about it, and Matt didn't have to do it himself – a simple phone call to one of his centres of influence meant more business for everyone involved.

HR, IT, succession issues, estate planning – the opportunities are endless, but only if you're alert to them. Throughout his long career, Mark has had many discussions with clients who've had their businesses for decades. He can feel when a client is starting to wonder, *What's next?* Of these clients, many have no idea how to exit their businesses or who will succeed them. One of his clients had a power of attorney appointed for their business, as advised by a legal firm. This has become common practice so if something happens to your client, they have a clear and concise plan for the business. Who runs the business? Who makes the key decisions? Who pays the bills and orders the stock? Mark knows the importance of having a great legal team within your contacts so your clients can manage their businesses in the most legal and ethical way, especially upon their exit.

Once again, that means having a system in place to make sure you're aware of what's going on in your clients' businesses – for example, by revisiting their needs reviews and gap analyses on a regular 6- or 12-month cycle. In our observation, only around 5 percent of advisory firms do this, and those that do get great results and returns.

Prophet Gap is a great way to enact these systems so you can stay on top of your clients' goals. Finding out what the client does or does not know about the following areas allows you to identify alternative ways to assist and add value. This can be through work you undertake in house or through introducing a specialist:

- Personal financial control
- Business debt
- Death and disability
- Business direction and planning
- HR and employment law
- Business succession planning
- Job satisfaction
- Work-life balance
- Staff engagement
- Structuring
- Asset protection
- Competitive advantage, marketing, and innovation
- Process improvement

To maximise the potential of these engagement opportunities for your firm, you'll need to plan for these scenarios in advance and take the time to develop either in-house expertise or a strong referral network.

NETWORK MAKES THE DREAM WORK

How do you expand your network to accommodate the myriad of situations your clients find themselves in? It's all about who you know and, in turn, who they know. First up – find and join a local referral group (but don't expect to receive a referral from them for a minimum of 6 months). The aim is to find like-minded people whom you can have discussions with to understand how they can help your clients. The more you understand about how they can help, the more you'll see opportunities for your clients to improve their businesses or personal financial situations. Similarly, the more that other people in the network see how hard you work for your clients, the more clients they'll refer to you.

Search for and join local referral groups on social media, talk to your contacts and see if they can introduce you to people within their network, and be proactive in vetting your own new contacts. Matt has a networking group he meets with each fortnight, going on to host a lunch every 3 months so he can further expand his network. Both Matt and Mark absolutely love connecting their clients with their network. It's their favourite part of the process and has proved to be incredibly rewarding for everyone involved.

Matt has a set of lawyers who provide differing attitudes, which he can match with his clients' personalities. If a client needs a lawyer who's aggressive and straightforward, he can match them with the right person. If a client needs a family lawyer who's focused on producing an amicable outcome, once again, he can match them with the right person. Matt even has three mortgage brokers within his network who suit different clients. In fact, overall, he has a large and diverse referral network. Diversity makes it easier to match clients and their specific needs to the right specialists.

Matt explains how networking strengthened his relationship with a client. His client had a family member who found themselves owing a significant amount of money to the ATO, all while still being legally married to his estranged partner. Matt offered to help, meeting with the client's family member, now his new client, along with a bankruptcy specialist to discuss the next steps. As there were children involved, he also organised a follow-up meeting with a family lawyer, a friend of Matt's from university who practises family law and was ready and willing to provide guidance, including how to handle child support obligations and how the client should communicate with his ex-partner. After two meetings, the client mentioned how lucky he felt that Matt knew the right people to help. Matt made those introductions and was the lifeline in a moment of crisis. He was able to provide a clear and concise path and lift some of the weight off his client's shoulders just by introducing him to two people.

Mark doesn't want you to get comfortable. In fact, he encourages you to step out of your comfort zone, getting out there and forming that network yourself. Go to events. Reach out to friends and friends of friends. Attend monthly meetings where people in your business sphere exchange details. Reach out to people you've worked with in the past. Show up for your contacts when called on. Find and foster those professional relationships. See a problem? Solve it! The key to succeeding at step six is to face it with an inquisitive and problem-solving mindset.

Now onward to the final step of the Enabler™ process, where you identify, generate, and capitalise on new business opportunities for you and your clients.

STEP 7

GENERATE NEW BUSINESS OPPORTUNITIES

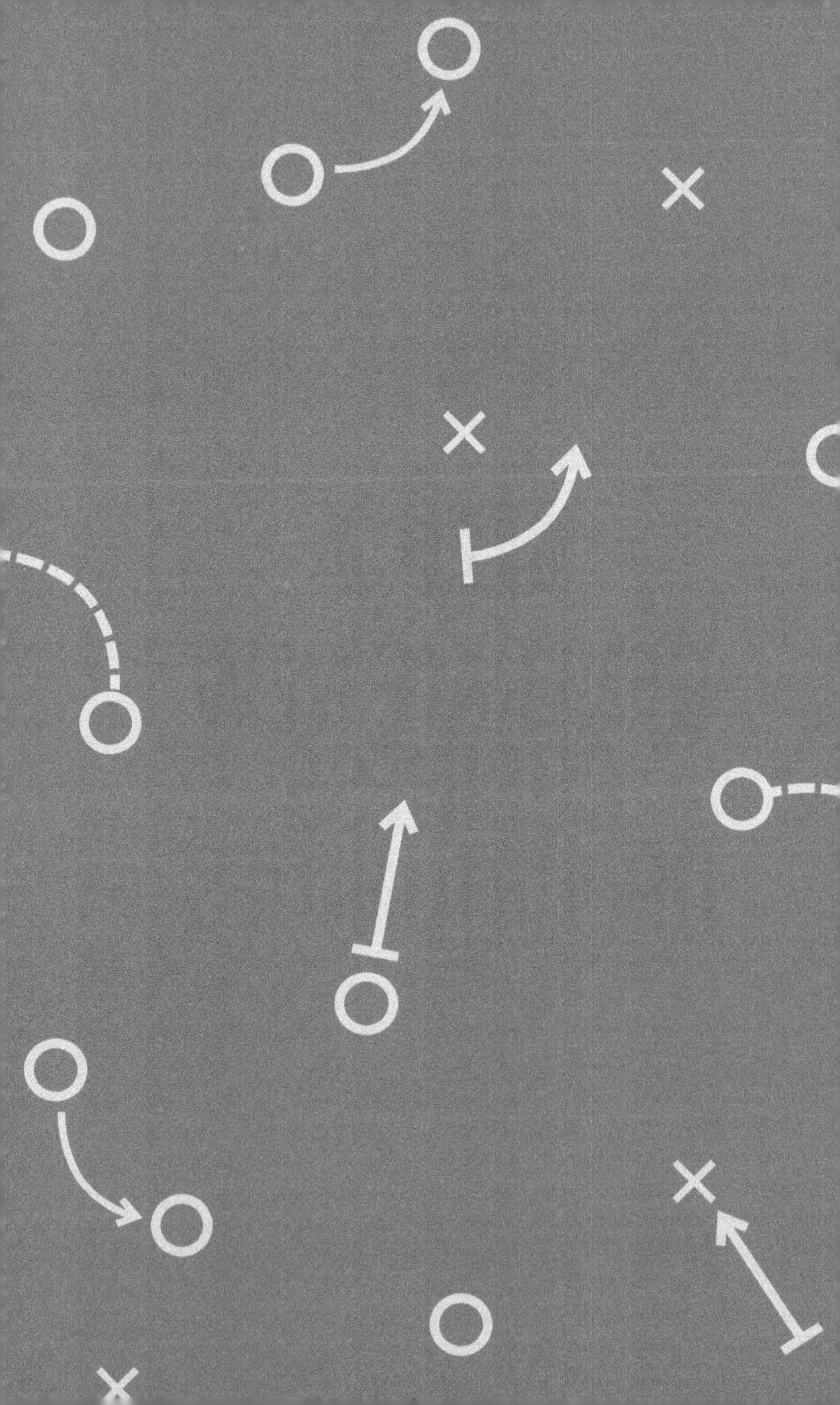

How would you like to see the financial impact of key business decisions before you make them? Step seven is all about forecasting those for your client (and yourself). Many clients make decisions based on nothing more than speculation and then come to you after the fact, leaving you in the lurch with few options to advise them. However, by showing your clients the future impact of decisions they may make today, you can generate new business opportunities and, importantly, ensure they're pursuing the right ones.

"YOUR JOB AS A BUSINESS ADVISOR IS TO BE THE GOALKEEPER, ENSURING NOTHING SLIPS PAST OR MOVES OUT OF REACH FOR YOU OR YOUR CLIENT."

As you gain more experience in business advisory, you'll come to a point where you can see the issues before they've materialised, and you'll be able to reach out to your clients prior to a problem arising so they have the best chance of avoiding trouble. It's hard to undo the past, but with your help, your clients can make smart decisions to benefit them in the future.

A great example of this is forecasting the volume of revenue and quality of work a new staff member will bring to your client's business. Before employing a new staff member, you can encourage your client to assess if a candidate's experience and expertise will benefit their business. How much additional revenue and profitability will this staff member generate for your client? What specialists will your client need when hiring someone new? Your advice prior to your client making their decision shows them they're supported during the hiring process.

But … how can a client ask for your assistance if they don't know you offer this service? You have to promote your services, and you have to promote yourself, which can be both challenging and rewarding. Promotion tactics include:

- Hold a seminar to show your clients what you can do for them
- Market yourself and your business using social media and digital marketing tools
- Have scenario-planning meetings with existing clients

- Check in with your clients and explain any additional services you offer

If you're willing to put in the work, the opportunities are endless. After working with your clients and developing partnerships, you'll be their go-to specialist for any business decisions. Their trust in you will mean new business opportunities not just for them but also for you.

When meeting with his clients, Matt likes to ask them what decisions they plan to make in the next month, 3 months, 1 year. Also, what's the biggest hurdle they'll need to overcome in the future? Your clients will usually give you something to work with, presenting an opportunity for you to offer your services.

Matt had a client who was expecting their third child within a matter of months. Upon meeting with them, he queried what their plan was for their business once postpartum, asking questions like, "How much leave will you require?" The client told Matt that 12 weeks would be ideal, being the most challenging period after welcoming a new baby into the world. Matt hit the ground running, tying up loose ends within their business over the following months so they could take 12 weeks off and not have to worry about how the business was running.

DEVELOP A MARKETING MINDSET

As an accountant, sales and marketing probably isn't your first love. But if you want your advisory practice to flourish, you'll need to develop a mindset of constantly looking for opportunities, marketing them effectively, and proactively selling them to your clients. Matt doesn't market his business as anything other than advisory services. His clients may still ask if they do tax work (which they do), but Matt knows that his passion and his greatest success lie within business advisory.

Mark agrees – he knows that most accountants focus on their front-end offerings. However, good practices diversify their income and opportunities, putting advisory services at the top of the food chain. Mark wants you to pitch value to your clients, and support the process with your compliance work. All tax work is simply taking yesterday and converting it into a format that suits the tax office. You need to shift your thought process to look to the future, which is the core focus of business advisory.

It's not just about *you* changing *your* thinking – you can change your clients' mindsets as well. Matt had a client who was complaining about their business activity statement (BAS) going up in price. Matt reframed this complaint to his client by letting them know the increased cost was due to their business improving in revenue. This was a really healthy indicator for the business! Success breeds consequence, and that consequence is tax. Who better to manage your clients' tax and financial outcomes than you?

In our experience, the place to start your marketing plan is with your existing client base. As we've described, once your firm is ready to start offering advisory services, it's a matter of deciding which clients are most suitable, identifying their needs, working with them, and expanding your offer to them in your regular 3- or 6-month review meetings. Over and above that, you'll want to get the word out about your advisory service so you can grow your fee base with new clients too.

Matt rebranded his business specifically to attract clients that were more focused on business advisory rather than tax work. He also wanted to distinguish himself from other accountants in his local area. He found that the concept of celebration worked wonders for him. Celebrating in a monthly or quarterly newsletter. Celebrating at team meetings, on social media, and on their website. Creating a confident and positive atmosphere really intrigued clients and resulted in more advisory work.

You should review your current marketing tools: your website, social media pages, seminars. How can you use them to promote your advisory services? Get out there and shout from the highest mountains that you're the accounting firm of choice. You're not only marketing yourself; you're also helping your clients, and their word-of-mouth reviews of your work are worth their weight in gold. When they mention your services to their friends, it's likely to generate new business, as you've set yourself apart from accountants who only focus on compliance work.

INTRODUCING THE LIPS METHOD

When seeking to set your firm apart from the competition, the LIPS method can help.

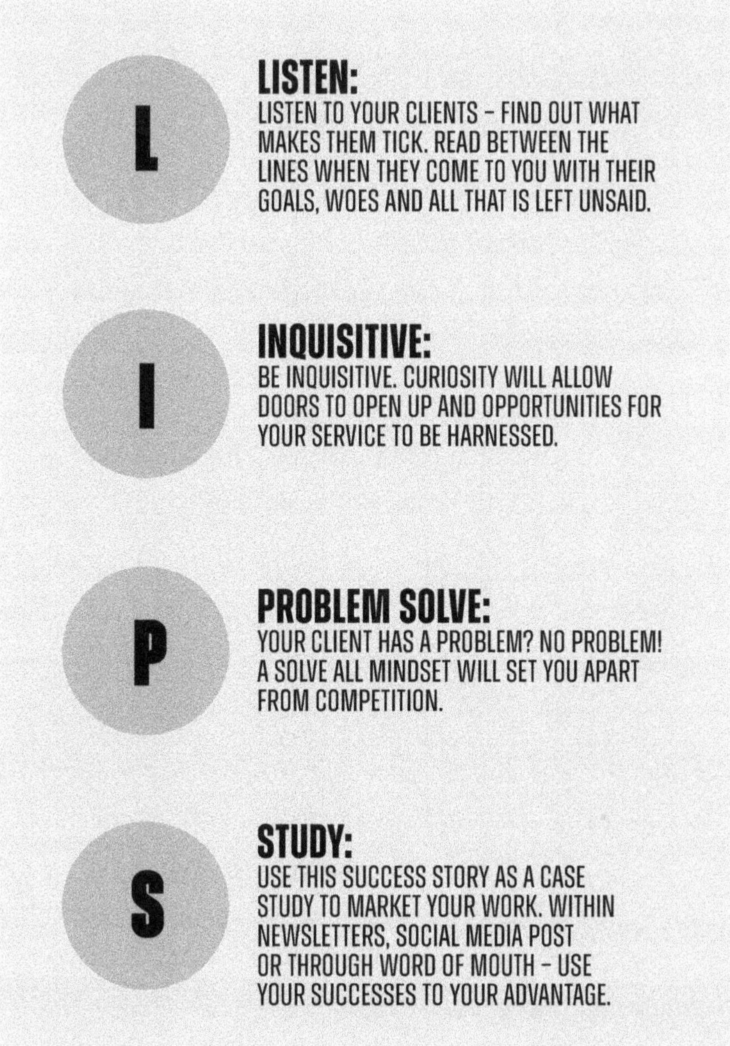

GET CREATIVE WITH YOUR MARKETING

Matt approached his clique of specialists and created a website that combines all their separate businesses. Property Investor Centre is a hub where potential clients can access Matt's advisory and accounting services, conveyancers, mortgage brokers, property investors, and more. While they market themselves as one business, it's actually five businesses coming together, and it only costs Matt $50 per month to cover the web hosting. A little bit of cash for a lot of long-term gain. This allows Matt to have targeted conversations with potential clients looking for relevant services.

Mark recommends keeping your marketing holistic. Embrace the combination of marketing tools at your disposal and foster your existing relationships. Mark's best referrals across his career have come from happy clients. Maintaining strong partnerships with your contacts means those businesses, clients, and specialists are more likely to refer work your way. Don't leave any loose ends. Have a website that backs up your services, and maintain your presence both online and in real life as a trusted source for business advisory.

Here are several sales and marketing strategies you might want to employ to generate interest in your advisory work among new and existing clients:

- Use social media, your website, and email newsletters to continually position yourself as a trusted specialist advisor. Use your success stories as case studies, and don't be shy about including them in your online presence.
- Get actively involved in the industry and community that generates most of your work – attend events, put your hand up to speak at conferences, and sponsor community initiatives.
- Foster relationships with those in your centres of influence. We find that as you get better known around town for your business advisory work, the influencers in your community want to work with you – the banks, finance brokers, real estate agents, lawyers, and so on.
- At tax time, advertise your compliance work at a fixed price when bundled with a needs review process to open the door to advisory engagements.
- Create marketing material that ties in with the seven steps of the Enabler™ process.

- Continually remind your clients that you can help them predict the financial implications of business decisions in advance using your scenario-planning software.

- Hold a firm seminar to open your clients' minds to the possibilities, either using in-house expertise or featuring an industry expert like Mark Holton (Mark often speaks on behalf of our clients on topics such as "Do you want to know the financial consequences of your business decisions before you make them?") Please contact us at www.m2academy.com.au if you'd like more details

Peter Fowler from Collins Hume explains how he uses some of the steps of the Enabler™ process in his marketing material:

We might write an article on valuations or business coaching, or something that doesn't give the customers a lot of information. It creates a bit of a disturbance. And then at the bottom, it will usually have an offer. Either for our workshop or for a free consultation or a free needs analysis or something like that, something that's low-cost and could get us a foot in the door with the client.

Domenic Stramandinoli from Nexis Accountants shares his experience successfully marketing advisory services:

You've got to be proactive. You've got to go out and get your own leads and centres of influence … We did a lot of seminars with the Canberra and Queanbeyan Business Councils, which created a lot of leads … We also attended industry groups, and we went and spoke to a number of clients who then put us in touch with their industries as well. So there are a number of formal marketing channels, and then a lot of it is word of mouth, coming from the internal client base.

READY TO BECOME A FEARLESS ADVISOR TO YOUR CLIENTS? WE CAN HELP!

Are you now fired-up, motivated, and ready to launch business advisory services in your firm? This book and the seven-step Enabler™ process provide all the tools you need to achieve success for both you and your clients. Need some extra guidance to ensure you make nothing but winning decisions moving forward? We can help.

Our mission is to help you turn your practice into a great business. One that delivers outstanding financial returns and that you and your team love being part of. All our services are developed with exactly that goal in mind.

- Join your peers at one of our leadership or advisory events and come away having made a solid start on a business advisory implementation plan that you can take back to the office and start working on immediately.

- Engage one of our specialist consultants to advise you on the IT infrastructure, business processes, or sales and marketing model that will work best for your firm as it establishes itself as an advisory services provider.

- Enlist our expertise to conduct firm reviews for succession planning or due diligence for mergers and acquisitions.

Connect with us today, and together we'll turn your practice into a phenomenal business.

AFTERWORD

For years I have watched accounting firms navigate constant change as automation, AI, and rising client expectations reshape the industry.

Compliance continues to be essential, and firms now build on that foundation by offering deeper guidance and forward-looking support. Clients want someone in their corner. They want clarity that helps them look ahead, make confident decisions and feel supported in the moments that matter.

Advisory is becoming the heartbeat of firms that want to stay relevant, profitable and trusted.

Yet the same pattern appears again and again. Firms understand why advisory is important but struggle with how to build it. They want to deliver deeper support, but capacity, confidence, and clarity often stand in the way.

Technology can free up time and give better visibility, although it will not create a strong advisory engine on its own. The firms that succeed combine smart tools with structure, intent and a culture that backs meaningful, year-round conversations.

That's why this book has never been more relevant. In *The Fearless Advisor's Playbook*, Matt Feehan and Mark Holton reveal a practical seven step system that gives firms a simple and repeatable way to move from reactive work to proactive advisory. The process covers discovery, planning, forecasting, needs analysis, scenario modelling and steady follow through.

It turns advisory into something reliable, scalable, and consistent.

Matt and Mark's approach is grounded and real. Between them they have worked with thousands of firms, and they understand the common roadblocks. Confidence. Time. Knowing where to start. The fear of getting it wrong. The challenge of shifting habits inside a busy practice. Their examples and tools are drawn from hands-on experience rather than theory.

They also remind us that advisory is both technical and human. It is not about generating more reports. It is about curiosity, trust and honest conversations. It is about helping business owners move forward with clarity and feel supported in the decisions that shape their future.

If you are reading this, you already know your firm has more to offer. This book will help you turn that intention into action. Work through the steps. Bring your team with you. Build capability steadily and with purpose. The impact on your clients and on your firm can be significant.

Matt and Mark have created a resource the profession genuinely needs. My hope is that you put it to work and see the difference it can make.

TRENT MCLAREN

Co-Founder of Vinyl

Founder of Journey & The Firm

ABOUT THE AUTHORS

MARK HOLTON OAM

Mark Holton (FCPA) has more than 40 years' experience as an accountant and tax agent in practice. He is a director of Smithink Advisory trading as Mark Holton Consulting.

Mark has developed specialised skills in corporate presentations and training, with extensive experience in both private and public sector industries in Australia, New Zealand, United Kingdom, and North America. He is also a respected consultant in taxation and business management, in particular value-added services implementation and administration using key business advisory systems and software.

Mark is a lively and entertaining speaker, whether as a keynote addressing large audiences, the facilitator of a partner retreat or conference, or the leader of a professional development course. His engaging speaking style means his audiences are always alert and entertained at his events.

Mark holds a Master of Commerce degree as well as several postgraduate qualifications in accounting and management. He also has a degree in Adult Education and an Advanced Diploma of Financial Planning.

Mark is the honorary treasurer of Ronald McDonald House Greater Western Sydney, a role he has held for over 30 years. He is also the vice chair of Bendigo Bank East Gosford and Districts and director of finance at the New South Wales Rugby League Referees Association.

MATT FEEHAN

Matt Feehan is the managing director of Three Rivers Group and founder and CEO of Prophet Gap, working with business owners and accounting firms to build better, more sustainable businesses.

With over 20 years of experience in public practice, Matt works closely with small to medium-sized and family-run businesses to align their financial performance with what they actually want from life. He also partners with sole practitioner accounting firms to help them run more efficient, profitable and valuable practices.

Matt is an advisory-first accountant who believes compliance is just the scorecard – not the game. His focus is on understanding what clients are trying to build and using financial insight to help them get there.

He's known for building strong, long-term relationships and for translating numbers into practical decisions that drive real outcomes.

A CPA with a double degree in accounting and law, Matt is a regular speaker who brings a grounded perspective to his practical insights – delivering no-fluff advice from someone still doing the work every day.

JESSICA TONELLI (AUTHOR)

Jessica Tonelli has been a freelance writer for over 15 years, working with local and internationally recognised publications on a range of topics, including music, finance, and accounting.

Jess founded a digital marketing company called Canyon Digital located in Bellingen, NSW, servicing clients from across the country and overseas. She believes in creating engaging and informative content that elevates businesses to their potential, and she loves working closely with her clients to develop impactful marketing strategies.

AUDIOBOOK

Great news! *The Fearless Advisor's Playbook* is also available in audio format. Jump onto your favourite audiobook platform now and check it out.

APPENDIX

THE RIGHT TOOLS FOR THE JOB

Identify what's important to the client

Prophet Gap – www.prophetgap.com

Mark Holton 10 x 10 Needs analysis –
www.markholton.com.au/resources

B Star RVDA – www.bstar.com.au

Administrative Tools

Pipedrive – www.pipedrive.com

Monday.com – www.monday.com

Hubspot – www.hubspot.com/products/crm

Budgeting and Cashflow

Adviserli – www.advisorli.com

Jazoodle – www.jazoodle.com

Castaway – www.castawayforecasting.com

Business Value Indication

The Benchmarking Group – www.benchmarking.com.au

B Star – https://bstar.com.au

Scenario Planning

Adviserli – www.advisorli.com

Cash Flow Story – www.cashflowstory.com

Jazoodle – www.jazoodle.com

Dashboarding

Fathom – www.fathomhq.com

Spotlight Reporting – www.spotlightreporting.com

Cash Flow Story – www.cashflowstory.com

Adviserli – www.advisorli.com

10 BY 10 NEEDS REVIEW
GOOD CLIENT CONVERSATIONS DON'T HAPPEN BY ACCIDENT.

These questions are designed to get people talking, because when clients talk, you find out what's really going on. The concerns that matter most rarely come out first. Listen carefully, follow the thread, and ask the follow-up that digs a little deeper.

Avoid anything that can be answered with a yes or no, and shape these questions to suit your client and your own natural style.

$ BUSINESS PROFITABILITY IMPROVEMENT

1. What has been the greatest success you have had in your business over the past 12 months?
2. What part of your business would you look to change, if you could, over the past 12 months?
3. What key financial and non-financial ratios or KPI's do you need to measure to create and monitor success?
4. Describe the trends in sales, margins and stock levels on your business?
5. Do market conditions impact on your sales and

profitability? Describe how you have tried to address this in the past.

6. How can you improve the effectiveness of your marketing activities?

7. How do you plan and monitor success in your business? Are there any obstacles that hinder this planning process?

8. What level of return do you expect your business to generate over the next year? How do you measure return against the cost of borrowings?

9. How do people's challenges impact on the success of your business?

10. What improvements can be implemented to improve the level of customer service? What strategies have you employed that have worked in the past?

BUSINESS CONDITIONS

1. What external factors impact the performance of your business? What can you do to capitalise on the opportunities and minimise the risk brought about by these factors?

2. Describe the difference between your business

and your competitors' businesses. What are they doing better than you? What are you doing better than them?

3. Looking forward what is the potential for demographic changes to impact your business? e.g. people living longer, immigration, people getting married and having children later, city vs regional growth etc.

4. What is the potential for new competitors to emerge in the next 5 years? Where might they come from?

5. What issues keep you awake at night when you think about your business?

6. Describe how government policies can impact your business? How do you feel about the current policy debates?

7. How would you describe your business compared to 5 years ago? What is harder? What is easier? Where have you had your greatest success? What has not gone well?

8. Describe how you feel about the future of your business.

9. What have been the impacts of changing input costs for your business? How do you see these input costs changing in the future?

10. How likely is it that overseas competition will increase? Why do you have that view? What can you do about it if it is likely?

🧠 MARKETING

1. What marketing activities are working for you? Not working for you?

2. How does your marketing differ to your competitors?

3. If you had more resources available what additional marketing activities would you undertake?

4. Describe the impact your website has had on your business?

5. How would you like to improve your website?

6. How do you feel about using social media to market your business? If you are – how could you improve the impact of your social media activity?

7. What new markets are potential opportunities for you? What is holding you back accessing those markets?

8. How would your team describe your marketing? How would they suggest it could be improved?

9. Tell me about your most successful marketing

campaign? Least successful marketing campaign?

10. How could you improve your brand recognition?

 # HUMAN RESOURCES

1. How do you think you could make your people more effective?

2. What are you doing to ensure that you're complying with all the industrial relations regulations?

3. Describe how you are measuring and monitoring the performance of your team?

4. How do you feel the management of your employees might be improved?

5. How would you describe the morale of your employees? How do you think morale could be improved?

6. What benefits do your employees receive? What additional benefits have you considered?

7. Who are your main competitors for labour? How can you effectively compete with these competitors to get the labour you need?

8. Describe your process to review employee performance and to provide feedback. What have been your key findings out of this process?

9. How might technology change impact the type of people you may need to employ in the future?

10. How would your employees respond to the question – "What is it like working here?"

🖧 TECHNOLOGY AND PROCESS

1. How has technology change been impacting on your business? How should you be responding to these changes?

2. What is impacting the productivity of you and your people causing them to be less efficient?

3. How could customer service be improved?

4. What technologies have your competitors implemented that is giving them a competitive advantage?

5. Describe how a complete review of your business processes, where you rethink how you do things and the technology you use, might impact the business.

6. How do you feel about moving more of your technologies to the cloud with the potential positive impact on cost and efficiency?

7. How could you more effectively capture and share

the knowledge in the heads of your key people?

8. How might mobile technologies change your business and how you engage with customers?

9. What extra information about your business, your products or your customers might enable you to have a more effective business?

10. How might your business differ in 5 years compared to how it is today?

💼⑤ FINANCE

1. What additional funding will be needed to meet your current and future plans? How much will you need and when will that be?

2. Will any existing funding needed to be rolled over in the next 12 to 18 months? What plans do you have in place to manage this?

3. To what extent does your understanding of current lending covenants and risk rates apply to your financing?

4. What new financing arrangements have you considered or put in place recently?

5. What varying types of finance available to you and your business have you considered putting in place?

6. What do you think about personally funding the additional financing needs of the business?

7. What opportunities have you considered to raise capital and/or introduce new partners or investors?

8. To what extent will loan funding help your business grow?

9. How will your budget and cash flow impact future financing?

10. How will the loan will be repaid if something was to happen to you or the business?

⚖️ RISK MANAGEMENT

1. What would happen to your family and business if you passed away?

2. What would happen to your family and business if you were incapacitated or you got sick for a significant period of time?

3. How does your current will meet your objectives if you passed away?

4. Do you have an estate plan in place and is there sufficient protection for beneficiaries – please describe?

5. What concerns do you have regarding your fellow

partners/directors and or shareholders?

6. How do your partnership/shareholder agreements ensure that your objectives are met if you passed away, became incapacitated or had an issue with your fellow partners and or shareholders?

7. How is business valuation built into these documents? If not do you believe this is a critical step forward?

8. Can you describe what 'cross cover' insurances that you currently have and their sufficiency to meet anticipated risks?

9. Will your other insurances manage current and future risks – how so?

10. What are your three biggest business risks and how do you plan to manage them?

✅ SUCCESSION PLANNING

1. How long can you continue to work in your business before wanting to get out?

2. What is your plan for your business as you scale down?

3. Do you have a smart succession plan to assist you to transition out of the business – please describe?

4. Do you want to sell your business? If so how much do you think the business is worth now?

5. How much do you need your business to be worth in the future to be able to walk away and feel that you received a good return on investment?

6. How do you feel about selling equity to your senior management team?

7. What is your staff and management succession plan after your leave the business?

8. Are systems and procedures well documented in order for a new owner to assume control and continue to run the business?

9. Do your clients come to you because of the business and its products and services, or because they have a connection with a specific staff member or owner?

10. Describe how you can you make yourself and other key people in your business dispensable?

RETIREMENT

1. What does a comfortable retirement look like to you and your family?

2. What investments do you currently have and do you think that they are sufficient?

3. What is your current net wealth and how do you intend to develop it from now until retirement?

4. Have you considered when you are going to retire? If so when do you think that may be?

5. Have you considered what education funding goals need to be set? If not what do you think they may be?

6. What other health, living and holiday funding goals need to be set to ensure your retirement is sustainable?

7. What is the proper spending rate from your savings, and what economic factors does it depend on?

8. Would you consider retiring later if it was necessary to attain your financial goals?

9. How long will your money last if you stop working today?

10. Taking everything into account is your retirement income plan sustainable?

😄 FAMILY/PERSONAL

1. What are your goals, hopes and dreams for your family and yourself?

2. What is concerning you regarding your family?

3. What changes will be happening (or you would like to see happen) on the family front in the next few years?

4. What are you doing to ensure you're getting enough of a break to recharge your batteries?

5. What are you doing to ensure you stay healthy and keep stress under control?

6. What are the obstacles making it hard for you to achieve your goals?

7. How happy are you with the performance of your business and the return for your effort?

8. If you had more personal time what would you do with it?

9. What is frustrating you?

10. How could family life be improved?

ENDNOTES

1   Bullo G, Chinnery A, Roche S, Smith E, and Wallis P (2024) 'Small Business Economic and Financial Conditions', *Reserve Bank of Australia*, accessed 13 October 2025, https://www.rba.gov.au/publications/bulletin/2024/oct/pdf/small-business-economic-and-financial-conditions.pdf; Small Business Commissioner (29 April 2025) 'Navigating Rising Costs and Tariffs: Strategies for Small Business Resilience', *NSW Government*, accessed 13 October 2025, https://www.smallbusiness.nsw.gov.au/news-podcasts/news/navigating-rising-costs-and-tariffs-strategies-for-small-business-resilience.

2   Bremmer I (2006) *The J Curve: A New Way to Understand Why Nations Rise and Fall*, Simon & Schuster.